Tour de France:
The Inside Story

Making the World's
Greatest Bicycle Race

Les Woodland

McGann Publishing
Cherokee Village, Arkansas

This book was originally published in a slightly altered form in 2009 as *Tourmen: The Men Who Made the Tour de France*. It has been updated to reflect the events that have happened since the original publication.

Published by McGann Publishing
P.O. Box 576
Cherokee Village, AR 72525
USA
www.mcgannpublishing.com

McGann
Publishing

ISBN 978-0-9859636-3-7
Printed in the United States of America

Their legs, like giant levers, will power onwards... their muscles will grind up the kilometres, their broad chests will heave with the effort of the struggle, their hands will cling to their handlebars; with their eyes they will observe each other ferociously; their backs will bend forward in unison for barbaric breakaways; their stomachs will fight against hunger, their brains against sleep. And at night a peasant waiting for them by a deserted road will see four demons passing by, and the noise of their desperate panting will freeze his heart and fill it with terror.

—Henri Desgrange, organizer of cycle races

Table of Contents

Introduction 7

Part One: Départ Fictif 9

One: A Funny Thing Happened at the Bike Track..........11
Two: The Barnum of Cycling 17
Three: A Private War 25

Part Two: Départ Réel 33

One: You Go Instead, Petit Géo...35
Two: Who Are You, Henri Desgrange? 41
Three: A Stern Father 49
Four: You Are But Mere Babies...55
Five: Les Forcats de la Route...61
Six: The Swoop of the Kingfisher 67
Seven: My Race Has Been Won by a Corpse.................. 73

Part Three: Echappée Matinale 79

One: An Era Dawns..81
Two: Foreigners Abroad 87
Three: The People's Race 93
Four: Tour of Dreams 99
Five: The Enigma of 1940.. 105

Part Four: La Chasse 111

One: Out of the Shadows 113
Two: The Fabulous Fifties............................. 117
Three: The War of the Gods 121
Four: The I of the Needle............................. 127
Five: Everyone Takes Something...................... 133
Six: My Sponsor Right or Wrong 139

Part Five: Flamme Rouge 145

One: The Eagle Has Landed............................ 147
Two: Welcome to My World 155
Three: Mr Smiley, Mr Grumpy, Mr Cheat.................... 163

Part Six: L'arrivée 169

One: Into the Future 171
Two: ...Darkly..................................... 175
Three: The Lone Star State 179
Four: The Leader of the Pack........................ 185
Five: Shooting Stars................................. 193
Six: English Not Spoken Here........................ 199
Seven: English Most Definitely Spoken Here............... 205
Eight: Under New Management.......................211

Part Seven: Le roi est mort, vive le roi! 217

Index..223

Over The Hills And Far Ago

Just an hour's ride from here—it's over two big hills and the flesh is weak—lies the route of the first Tour de France. The riders stopped in Moissac, where there is no statue to them but there is one to local grapes and clean water, and there they signed the control sheet at the Hôtel Luxembourg. It's still there, on a bend in the road. From there they took the Garonne valley towards Bordeaux and passed through the little town of Valence d'Agen. Its only other part in Tour history is that the field got off and walked across the line there in protest at being woken up early for three races in a day, after a mountainous time the stage before. That was 1978.

The funny thing is that few people in Valence remember that strike, with its thrown tomatoes and Bernard Hinault jumping over the barriers to land a fist on those who'd thrown them and the mayor shrieking at strikers that they'd ruined his day. Even fewer care that the souls of 1903 passed that way on the greatest adventure they or cycling had known.

It's impossible now to see where they went. In their day, traffic would have crossed the heart of the town, but whether along what is now the *route nationale* or nearer the canal, I don't know.

They were an experiment, those riders, rats in a laboratory. Most sports evolve. Soccer began with mobs kicking a pig's bladder in the street. Marathon running came from carrying messages, the fact that the carrier dropped dead after the first not discouraging the mass runs of the 1970s. Cycling developed because it was fun to go fast on a bike and see who could do it best. But bicycle stage-racing, that was new.

There had been six-day races on the track, of course. It was they that inspired Géo Lefèvre to blurt out his idea about what, "if I understand you right, *petit Géo*", was a Tour de France. But track races were easy. You counted how many laps each rider finished in a week and you gave a prize to whomever managed most. Stopping at the end of each day and starting again together the next morning, that was different.

He was an odd cove, Henri Desgrange, but he invented a way. He invented bicycle stage-racing. It took decades to perfect it but he had nothing else to go on. His riders were genuine experiment creatures, too, because Desgrange wanted to inspire a weakling France, one which crumpled to the Prussians to the extent that Parisians ate rats and dogs as they were besieged.

"These men are human and yet they can achieve the inhuman," was his message. They were an inspiration, a target for others.

The more I thought about Dezzie, the more I came to appreciate how he had been shaped by his era and had shaped a sport because of it. And that, I began to see, went too for others. Sometimes they were officials, such as Jacques Goddet and Jean-Marie Leblanc; sometimes they were socialists giving the French two weeks' paid vacation; they were Jacques Anquetil and Raymond Poulidor, each the opposite of the other, each representing a self-image of France, of Europe, in the throes of change. Or they were Lance Armstrong.

If hardly anyone here in France knew even the shape of their country before the Tour de France, what else could we see in the way the race shaped France and France shaped the race? The nation and the race, they are abstract quantities. They need humans to give them life. And that's how I've told my tale.

Part One: Départ Fictif

Each day of the Tour de France, except those on which riders or teams set off individually, starts with a truce. The tradition began when riders had to find their own way. It was better to guide them out of town than have them get lost. In English, the truce is called the neutralized zone. In French, it is the "départ fictif", the false start.

1

A Funny Thing
Happened At The Bike Track

Nobody raced. They barely moved. They crept away and then all but stopped. The crowd shouted. It whistled in contempt. It waved its arms in the air and called it a disgrace. It was a national championship. It was the talk of Paris.

It was also the birth of bike racing. Oh sure, there'd been races before. They'd raced on the road and they'd raced on the track. But until then they'd just blasted away from the start and hoped to keep going. The idea that you could race only a thousand metres by starting slowly and getting slower was not only new but scandalous.

"The way the race finished just shows the result false," grumped the man from *La Bicyclette*.

So what happened? Well, we're going back a while, back to Paris of the late nineteenth century, to 1894. Tax records showed there were more than a million bicycles in France. Coca-Cola was on sale for the first time in America, stuffed with cocaine but with not a hint of alcohol, to satisfy Southern temperance. Someone called Pierre de Coubertin wanted to hold a planetary sports day and call it the Olympic Games. The French condemned a disagreeable man called Alfred Dreyfus, brought the country close to civil war but incidentally created the Tour de France. A French boffin discovered the virus that caused the Plague and blamed it on rats. And an American called Arthur Augustus Zimmerman was the world's first sprint champion on a bike.

It was right back then that six men reached the final of the French kilometre championship on the long-gone *vélodrome de Seine*, in a loop of the Seine at the end of the rue de Courcelles. Among them were Maurice Farman, who became a racing car driver and a pioneer of the airplane industry, Paul Médinger, the national sprint champion, and a man called Henri Debray who was always billed as Henri Antony. In the press seats A. M. Peragallo was reporting for *La Bicyclette*.

"The starting signal was given," he wrote, "and the six competitors, full of noble ardor, threw themselves into the race at…six kilometres an hour! Antony was in front. After the first banking, the speed dropped to five kilometres an hour, then to four, then to three, and men supposed to sprint their bikes ended up balancing them! Suddenly, something happened: M. Farman, tired of the business, gave two turns of the pedals, came out of the group and nipped into the lead. False alert! He slowed down and the procession restarted in single file…"

At first the crowd had been silent, puzzled. Now it grew cross. Bike-racers were the fastest people on earth and that's what folk had paid to see. Instead, here were six men riding slower than they could walk, looking at each other, even riding up and down the track. Larking about.

"M. Farman left the inside of the track and crossed it obliquely until he got to the outside by the balustrade," Peragallo recounted. "He looked round as though to invite his compatriots to take his place at the front of the group. Doing that, he had picked up speed. So, seeing the others had almost stopped and were therefore in the worst position to accelerate, he used his slight extra speed to accelerate suddenly, a bit before the second banking and, profiting from the slope, reached the middle of the bend with twenty metres' lead before any of his rivals had the chance to notice.

"This sudden flight provoked among the other five a moment of disarray that was easy to understand…"

Farman put his head down and went for the line. He had 40 metres but he weakened pedal by pedal. Only Louvet had the strength or wit to chase. He got to 20 metres but "at the start of the finish straight, exhausted after an effort lasting 600 metres and seeing he had no more chance of catching M. Farman, stopped suddenly." Antony couldn't see the point either and also gave up. Médinger went by both and came second.

What had happened? It was the birth of tactics. Probably nobody in the stands realized it and even Peragallo was puzzled. "The way the race finished just shows the result is false," he protested. "Louvet showed obvious superiority, not only over the five riders whom he led for more than a lap but equally over M. Farman, from whom he took back more than half the distance he had lost. Except that, like the hare in the fable, he had started too late!"

There is every reason to believe that Peragallo's weren't the only experienced if puzzled eyes at the track that day. He may have shaken hands on the way in with a bony-faced man with generous, fair eyebrows. Henri Desgrange had thrown in a job in law—legend says his bosses near the Place de Clichy objected to his cycling with bare calves—and begun writing cycling articles. He was the *vélodrome de Seine*'s director.

Desgrange was a serious young man, although his twin brother, Georges, was even more straight-faced. Georges looked like a defrocked monk and worked in contented boredom as a newspaper archivist. Henri, on the other hand, had fancied himself as a swimmer before realizing he moved like a struggling duck. He "battled in an altogether anarchic fashion to coordinate the beating of his legs with the alternate projection of his arms; he looked, alas, like a man drowning," said a witness.

He then took to running and, with some success, to cycling. The first race he saw was Bordeaux–Paris in 1891. That inspired him to join the *Amicale Vélo Amateur* after his twenty-fifth birthday. He gave racing a go, liked it but soon realized he was never going to be another Farman, still less a Zimmerman. He took a block and a half to get up to speed. He could write, though, and in an era of salesmen and charlatans he seemed to know what he was talking about.

Depeux-Dumesnil, the legal office where Desgrange worked, was twenty minutes' walk southeast along the rue Nôtre Dame de Lorette from the Folies Bergère, a cabaret famous for dancers who took off their clothes. The director was a man called Clovis Clerc. He knew about using entertainment to bring in crowds and he was interested when a round-faced and mustached Englishman, Herbert Duncan, said that what Paris needed was a bike track.

Herbert Osbaldeston Duncan has vanished from history. He was, though, a pretty good rider, one of the so-called English club who settled in Paris. The best known—the only known—these days is James Moore, the nineteen-year-old who won the big race at the world's first formal bike meeting and won Paris–Rouen, the first place-to-place race. It was an era, just before Zimmerman, when English riders were the best in the world.

Duncan was from an aristocratic family in London. He fit the Britsh image of an amateur as a man who didn't accept money because he

Herbert Duncan, the toff who shamed his family's amateur ideals: it was his idea to build Paris' first bike track.

already had enough of his own. His grandfather, George, was a cricketer, a steeplechase champion and a master of foxhounds. When Herbert, at eighteen, decided to turn professional anyway, society called him a traitor. If he dreamed of getting his folks to pay for a track, he was too late. So, at the suggestion of a rider and friend called Frédéric de Civry, who spoke impeccable English, he went to Clerc.

Clerc saw the possibilities in having the first track in Paris and chose a site close to the Porte Maillot, up from where the Arc de Triomphe now stands. He showed showman's flair. Paris had wowed three years earlier to a Wild West show put on by Buffalo Bill. Folk were still talking about him when Clovis said he'd build his track where Cody had set up his show and, what's more, name it after him.

Clerc knew striptease and enough about art to engage stars such as the American dancer Loie Fuller. But he knew nothing about bike tracks. For that, he employed this bright young journalist, Henri Desgrange, who appeared both knowledgeable and in need of a job. Desgrange designed a track in concrete, with gentle bankings and even trees towards the start of the finish straight. It was "a track worthy of its name", said a report. Among its habitués was the artist Toulouse-Lautrec.

The track's manager from 1895 was a playwright, Tristan Bernard, dark haired with a W-shaped mustache as wide as his face, who edited the *Journal des Vélocipédistes*. There are two stories about him. The first is that it was at the Buffalo that he had the idea of ringing a bell to announce the last lap. From there it spread to other sports. The other is that he was Jewish and that the Germans took him to the concentration camp at Drancy, in the Paris suburbs, and then to Auschwitz. With Germans at the door, he turned and saw his wife crying. "Don't cry," he said. "We were living in fear but from now on we will live in hope." His optimism had mixed foundations. Public uproar led to his being freed in 1943 but he died four years later of the treatment he had endured.

The Buffalo track in Paris—named after Buffalo Bill, designed by Henri Desgrange, paid for by striptease.

Desgrange was proud of his track and in May, 1893, a year before the puzzling kilometre championship, he set the world hour record there. There had been previous records but his 35.325 kilometres was first to be ratified by the International Cycling Association, forerunner of the *Union Cycliste Internationale*.

The Buffalo was quite the track. Georges Cassignard broke the world kilometre record there with 1 minute, 28 seconds. Of the next ten successful attacks on the hour, nine were on the Buffalo. It became so celebrated that Toulouse-Lautrec painted Tristan Bernard standing on the track, wearing plus-fours, his rustic beard sticking at an angle. The track stopped being used only because it was broken up for an aircraft factory in world war one.

Desgrange still holds the world 100-kilometre tricycle record and probably will for ever more. This man who wrote cycling snippets for anyone who'd pay joined Victor Goddet in 1897 in the management of a still newer track, the *Parc des Princes*. By then France was close to civil war over a man who may have been a spy. It was to have enormous consequences for France. It was to change Desgrange and Goddet and it was to create the Tour de France.

2
The Barnum Of Cycling

Between Desgrange's 1893 record and the start of world war one, the only hour record not set at the Buffalo was set in 1898 in Denver, Colorado. The man concerned was an American, Willie Hamilton. He rode 40.781 kilometres and held the record more than seven years before he was relieved by Lucien Petit-Breton.

Cycling was new in America. The first race had been only in May, 1878, over three miles in Beacon Park in Boston. The winner, C.A. Parker, belonged to the club at Harvard University, on the city's edge. The first bike dealer in the USA was also in Boston, as was the first club, the Boston Bicycling Club in 1878, and the first all-cycling newspaper, *Bicycling World*, in 1877.

What happened to C.A. Parker, or even what his names were, I don't know. It was too early for people to notice and they didn't. Not outside the sport, anyway. Within it, people took notice and in 1882 Boston built a board track in the New England Industrial Fair building. On it, Ralph Ahl was the first American to ride a mile in less than three minutes.

That proved irresistible. If people could ride that fast, a public could be wooed and charged for tickets. That occurred to Henry E. Ducker, from Buffalo on the banks of Lake Erie. The *New York Times* said on January 4, 1895: "Mr Ducker knows cycling from A to Z. He made himself famous in the eighties through his management of the Springfield race meets."

Ducker was another P. T. Barnum. The old showman was supposed to have boasted "There's a sucker born every minute." What he probably said was: "There's a customer born every minute." That was just how Ducker saw the world. And he thought it worth hiring architects and builders to build a track inside Hampden Park trotting track in

Springfield, Massachusetts, so he could hold three days of bike racing. That done, he went out and trumpeted up enthusiasm.

The *New York Times* obliged: "It is the opinion of the racing sharps that no meet this season, particularly in the East, will excel the 'diamond tournament,' which takes place at Springfield, Mass., next week. No cyclist with any pretension of speed will be absent from it…A majority of the prizes will be diamonds of a much better water than are usually given at race meets. The cracks know this, and perhaps this fact accounts for the large entry list which the Springfield races always have. Hampden Park, where the giants will struggle, is in the best possible condition. The course has been specially prepared, and is now exceedingly fast, as the recent speed trials there attest."

The paper put up a gold medal worth $50 for the fastest mile.

Nine thousand came on the first day. They watched the time for a mile fall to less than 2 minutes, 30 seconds, figures so stunning that cycling papers in Britain refused to print them. Next day eighteen thousand bought tickets to see more. Shops and factories closed for the duration. It was the start of a golden era in American cycling, known now only to diehards and historians. Yet for decades the greatest riders in the world were American and only when they had sorted out among themselves who was best would they bother going to Europe to see if anybody there was worth beating.

There were two sides to this, in historical order. The first, in Henry Ducker, was track riding. The first road race in America seems to have been in 1883, also in Springfield. The winner, a tall, graceful man called George M. Hendee, was given or gave himself the title of national champion. He rode 309 races, won 302 and could live on his prizes and endorsements. You could treat yourself to Hendee cigars and hats.

But the real money was on the track, which Hendee also rode. There was money for the brave, helmet-less, protection-less riders who rocketed behind motorbikes prone to disintegrate and kill both pacer and follower, and there was more for the sprinters, the short-distance riders. They, like Hendee, called themselves amateurs, even when they could live on what they won. The greatest American sprinter was the majestically named Arthur Augustus Zimmerman, happily known to most as Zimmy or Zim. The historian and author Peter Nye says: "He was reputed to win 47 races in one week, which probably included heats, from the quarter-mile to 25 miles, and finished some seasons with 100 or more victories."

Zimmerman, the son of a real estate broker in Camden, New Jersey, who'd already tried the long jump and triple jump as a student soldier, did not fit the role that the National Cyclists Union in Britain considered appropriate for an amateur. If that sounds irrelevant, British championships were the de facto championships of the world until, at the NCU's prompting, the International Cycling Association ran proper ones in 1893. Zimmy won the ICA championship too, still an amateur. And yet in just one race at Springfield he had won two horses, a harness and a buckboard, total value $1,000 or twice the average wage. Through that season, the *New York Times* said, he won 29 bicycles, several horses and carriages, half a dozen pianos, a house, land, furniture and "enough silver plates, medals and jewelry to stock a jewelry store." Only the naive would imagine he didn't sell them back to the promoters for their value in cash. The French writer, Pierre Chany, said he even won coffins.

The League of American Wheelmen insisted he was an amateur. The moment he stepped foot in Britain, bringing Raleigh bicycles he gave every sign of being paid to ride, the NCU named him a professional. That was supposed to change things at the International Cycling Association but it took no notice and the League of American Wheelmen simply told the British to stop being hoity-toity.

By 1896, three years after America established a formal professional class, there were 692 professional track riders in the US. But not all as rich as Zimmerman, nor as significant as Major Taylor. Taylor's success—which was considerable—was less significant than his color. He was black. He lapped the field in 880 yards in his first professional race, at Madison Square Garden. He was world champion in 1899, the second black man—after the boxer George Dixon in 1890—to become a world champion. "To American blacks," says Nye, "Taylor was a leading national figure." He was the first black American at the top, Dixon having been Canadian. "To Europeans, Taylor was treated with the deference of a champion athlete. But to most Americans, Taylor was just another black man in segregated society, regardless of his athletic success."

Which is true. There were plenty of black riders. But they raced among themselves. They weren't welcome in white society. Taylor was better treated in Europe than in his own land. But that doesn't mean he was always treated well. Henri Desgrange was so upset when he beat the home favorite, Edmund Jacquelin, at the *Parc des Princes* that he paid Taylor his $7,500 in 10 centime coins collected from the turnstiles. "Taylor needed a wheelbarrow to carry his winnings away."

The second side to American track racing spread over six days. It would have been a week had promoters been able to sell tickets on a Sunday.

The first near-continuous six-day race was in north London, in an arena 45 by 130 yards in an arching Victorian building called the Agricultural Hall. It's still there, in the depressed-but-reviving suburb of Islington, but now it's the Business Design Centre. Sweating cyclists shocked nobody because the neighbors had already been horrified by everything else. Britain's biggest dog show started there in 1891 and the locals began an Association for the Suppression of the Dog Show Nuisance in Popular Localities. People didn't know then about snappy titles.

One year a crocodile escaped and, mindful that crocodiles run at 30 miles per hour, there was some consternation. In 1864 lions grabbed an assistant as he poked straw into their cage and it wasn't, said a paper, "until the brutes were nearly blinded with the blows inflicted on their eyes that they were induced to relinquish their grip."

The area for a bike track may have been small but the hall was huge, an iron and glass arch like a railroad terminus. London's fogs got trapped within it and at one farming show people escaped but the cows suffocated. Only shorter legs and fresher air near the ground saved the pigs and sheep.

With that background, neighbors put on an air of pained tolerance when an American, Edward Payson-Weston, challenged an Irishman, Daniel O'Leary, to walk 500 miles. That was April 1877. Weston thought he was on to a good thing because in 1861 he'd walked 453 miles to see Abraham Lincoln's inauguration, an achievement blunted by turning up ten hours late and losing a $10,000 bet but winning a bag of peanuts. In 1867 he walked 1,200 miles from Portland, Maine, to Chicago in 26 days, winning back the $10,000 but being threatened by gamblers who'd bet he wouldn't do it. But it was O'Leary who lost this second challenge, getting to "only" 478 miles in 135 hours. The two decided to walk on, and on, and on, until one dropped. It was Weston, after 510 miles. O'Leary went home to Cork with the money, and there is a monument to him in nearby Rathbarry. Payson-Weston was still going strong at the age of 70 when he was hit by a cab in New York and never walked again.

London was dull in the nineteenth century and the attraction of sick and stumbling wretches pissing in their pants through exhaustion wasn't to be underrated. There were more walking races, pulling 20,000 spectators a day, and then someone hit on a six-day on bikes. In November 1878, Billy Cann rode 1,060 miles on a high-wheeler on a track that worked out at seven and a half laps to a mile.

Only four of the twelve racers were there when the race started. The rest joined in when they chose. The *Islington Gazette* reported: "At seven o'clock Markham fell heavily, and ten minutes later the Frenchman [Charles Terront, who won the first Paris–Brest–Paris] came on the track and rattled away in fine style, he at that point being seventeen miles and a half behind the leader, Phillips. The men kept well together for some time after this, but at twenty minutes past nine Markham again came to grief, Andrews falling over him. About half an hour afterwards Phillips and White fell heavily, and in a short time Phillips had to give up all idea of participating further."

Cann was billed, with no apparent justification, as Long Distance Champion of the North. That's where Sheffield appears to be to people in London. He led from the start on a 52-inch gear, lost seven pounds, and found the makers of his bike so grateful that they gave him a job. Less content was Terront, who disliked everyone and was disliked in return. He believed the British tried to trick him into sniffing a flower dosed with sleeping powder and that they wanted to poison his food. Instead of eating in the stadium, he went out to a café. The breaks cost him many of the 160 miles he finished behind Cann and he went home with £10.

The League of American Wheelmen tried to impose respectability by banning racing on the Sabbath. Organizers pointedly played hymns until midnight ticked up on Sunday night. Then the races started fast and struggled on. Ned Reading from Nebraska rode 260 miles in fourteen hours without getting off in New York in 1896; Charlie Miller slept just four and a half hours in the six days it took to cover 2,088 miles in 1897. The *Brooklyn Daily Eagle* said: "The wear and tear upon their nerves and their muscles, and the loss of sleep make them [peevish and fretful]. If their desires are not met with on the moment, they break forth with a stream of abuse. Nothing pleases them. These outbreaks do not trouble the trainers with experience, for they understand the condition the men are in."

Riders wobbled and fell. They became gibbering wrecks. The worse they got, the costlier the tickets became. The helpers, *soigneurs*, were paid by results. Riders started on black coffee, then cocaine or strychnine. The Canadian Torchy Peden, all 6 feet 3 inches and 220 pounds, told the journalist Alan Gayfer that he took so much strychnine by the end of his career that it would have killed a horse. Peter Nye says in *The Six-Day Bicycle Races* that soigneurs "did everything to keep racers going—if riders quit, they made no money and might never get another contract."

John Hoberman, a professor at the University of Texas who has made a life of researching drugs in sport, said: "The six-day bicycle races of the 1890s were de facto experiments investigating the physiology of stress as well as the substances that might alleviate exhaustion."

It was worth finishing "like a ghost, his face as white as a corpse, his eyes no longer visible because they'd retreated into his skull": New York paid Teddy Hale $5,000 when he won in 1896. The entire purse, in gold double-eagle dollars, weighed sixteen pounds.

Major Taylor hallucinated that he was being chased by a knifeman. Others fancied that spectators were stoning them. The *New York Times* protested in 1897: "An athletic contest in which participants 'go queer' in their heads, and strain their powers until their faces become hideous with the tortures that rack them, is not sport. It is brutality...Days and weeks of recuperation will be needed to put the Garden racers in condition, and it is likely that some of them will never recover from the strain."

In 1898, Charlie Miller rode as far in six days at Madison Square Garden as Alberto Contador in a month during the Tour de France of 2009. When that year New York and Illinois limited races to twelve of twenty-four hours, promoters obliged with two-man teams. Two could ride in relay for twenty-four hours and still race no more than half the day. Speeds went up, distances grew, crowds increased, money poured in. It started at Madison Square Garden in 1899. The French call a madison race "the American."

The hullabaloo was colossal. Several bands competed in parts of the track. Bing Crosby loved the crashes and was believed to pay the hospital bills of the injured. Peggy Joyce—an actress so wealthy that one of Cole Porter's songs bragged "My string of Rolls Royces is longer than Peggy Joyce's"—put up $200 whenever the action flagged. She handed over $1,000 when a band struck up "Pretty Peggy with Eyes of Blue." The historian Dick Swann remembered: "Fist-fights among the riders, the spectators and even on occasions the officials often provided extra entertainment for the capacity crowds." It took four policemen to separate one brawl between riders, he recalled.

Kyle Crichton wrote in *Colliers* in 1935: "The jams are the essence of the business. The riders will be going along at a good steady pace when one of them will suddenly dart out from the pack and pick up half a lap before the others are aware of what is happening. Instantly, the arena is bedlam. Down in the middle of the oval, the infield, the relief riders begin tumbling out of their bunks and on their wheels. The men on the saucer are now going at whirlwind speed, sticking close to the curves or riding high on the rim and swooping down at the turns, cutting through openings so narrow that the spectators can't even see them. The relief teams start on the flat, picking them up on the fly and touching them off like runners passing the baton in a relay race... The riders are making flying pickups and hitting the turns on high. One swerve, a bump, or a failure to crowd through an opening that suddenly closes will bring the pack down in a heap of tangled wheels and broken bones."

Babe Ruth earned $17,000 a year but Alf Goullet—pronounced like *roulette*—collected $11,500 in a week in 1914. Six-day organizers in the Jazz Age pocketed $250,000 a race. There was so much money that Europeans went west across the Atlantic but few Americans went east. Promoters weren't unaware of the Tour de France and they weren't about to help shoot their golden hen. As one history puts it: "They heard the constant complaining by citizens about reckless street racing in the big cities and used these complaints and their political influence to get laws passed to make road racing illegal in the eastern states. Many of these laws are still on the books today. This prevented the growth of road racing in the USA."

By the Great Depression, America had neither track nor road racing of any account. Which may explain why it took more than 60 years to make its mark on the Tour.

3

A Private War

Major Taylor retired in 1910, Zimmerman in 1905. They lived through the Dreyfus scandal and the birth of the Tour with no interest in either. Across the Atlantic few had even heard of Dreyfus. And yet it split France in a way impossible to imagine. The details—that a soldier was sent to Devil's Island on trumped-up charges of selling secrets to the

Alfred Dreyfus. Nobody ever said he was pleasant and many said he was guilty. Only after he'd been sent to Devil's Island did a nation admit it got it wrong.

Germans—are less important than the consequences. France split between right and left, town and country, intellectual and peasant, church and state. French mayors are not allowed to buy Christmas decorations; religious symbols are banned in public buildings including schools; France formally—and strictly—separates itself from all religions while hindering none...all because of the Dreyfus affair.

And it also brought about the Tour de France.

The roots are absurd. They grow from a horse-race course at Auteuil, a rich suburb of Paris. *Le tout Paris*—all Paris society—was there one summer day of June 1899. Among them was the president, Émile Loubet. An august, Victorian figure with a full beard, a lawyer, he was a moderate and not at all sure Dreyfus had done it. It made him a hated figure for the church, for capitalists and the army, all glad to see Dreyfus in a penal colony. One of those capitalists was Albert de Dion, often described as a count. Five years earlier he had won France's first car race, although he didn't get a prize because the car's steam engine needed someone to shovel coal.

Denying de Dion was chancy. He was a fanatical duelist. Few grievances were too trivial. He and sympathizers saw red when they spotted the president and one of them—possibly de Dion—brought his stick down sharply on Loubet's top-hatted head. De Dion got fifteen days in jail and a fine of 1,000 francs, which if he was the man who did it may suggest where the country's judges stood on Dreyfus.

Almost as ill-tempered when roused was Pierre Giffard, a round-faced man with thin dark hair who ran *Le Vélo,* the biggest of a dozen and a half sports papers. It began in 1892, mixing sports with news and a fair amount of comment. High in the comment in June 1899 was criticism of de Dion and the walking stick. If Giffard was cross then de Dion was crosser. He had spent a lot of money with Giffard, buying advertising for which he was convinced he was charged too much. He thought that especially because *Le Vélo* had been founded with the help of one of his rivals in the motor trade, Alexandre Darracq, and Darracq, he was sure, wasn't paying as much. More, de Dion was one of Giffard's largest shareholders, perhaps the largest.

The two argued as de Dion sat in La Santé jail. When de Dion got nowhere, he found allies in others of *Le Vélo*'s advertisers, notably André Édouard Michelin, the tire-maker. Together, they plotted to take Giffard down, first by wrecking his chance of entering politics, then by starting a paper of their own. And it wouldn't have politics in it.

Their problem was who to run it. There weren't many journalists not already involved with Giffard. But they knew of this Henri Desgrange who could write, who'd shown business sense in running the *Parc des Princes*, and who edited a publication called *Paris-Vélo*. Desgrange, then 35, had reason to push a stick in Giffard's wheels: *Le Vélo*, an eccentric publication, refused to take the *Parc des Princes* seriously and often didn't report races there. Desgrange was interested but he wasn't a man—as subsequent events proved—to take risks. He was good at taking credit but not at pushing the boat out.

Desgrange was in partnership with a businessman called Victor Goddet. Goddet, a quiet man not that enthused by sport, was majority shareholder at the *Parc des Princes*. Desgrange never did anything without his approval and often only at his suggestion. If de Dion wanted Desgrange then Goddet would be coming too. Desgrange wasn't yet the decisive, dictatorial man of later. He had an attack of nerves when de Dion asked him and Goddet to his office in the avenue de la Grande-Armée in Paris in April 1900.

"What are we going to do?" he asked as the two sat on a bench along the road. "Accept? Refuse?" Nearly three decades later, Desgrange remembered they went for the job after they realized that failing to would set Giffard on their tail and that "our poor *Parc des Princes* will be the loser in the battle."

It casts a different light on Desgrange. His image is of a lofty, autocratic man devastatingly critical of others. This, after all, was the man who used to wait outside the *Parc des Princes* to see who left without a shower and then published their names in a column headed "Dirty Feet". But he could be unsure, as we'll see when it comes to taking the Tour into the mountains—and, indeed, on to the road at all. It may have been this uncertainty that made *L'Auto* flop.

At this distance, it looks like the title was a problem. Why *L'Auto*, for a general sports paper? The answer is in the times. Cycling had wowed the leisured classes and cyclists filled Paris with joyful wobbling. "In London," said the authors Roderick Watson and Martin Gray, "the wealthy pedaled through the Parks with crowds thronging the walks to watch the stately spectacle. In Paris the Bois de Boulogne served the same purpose. The fashion papers avidly discussed the most suitable costume... Actresses posed by their bicycles. In America a few incredibly costly bicycles with gold and silver plating were bestowed by millionaires on their lady friends."

The man concerned, says the historian James McGurn, was Diamond Jim Brady, a financier and hefty eater who, "wanting ten gold-plated bicycles to present to his friends, had his own gold-plating plant built, had the job done, and the plant was torn down again. He gave his girlfriend, the celebrated comic opera singer Lillian Russell, a gold-plated bicycle with her monogram engraved on every gold part. It had mother-of-pearl handlebars, an enormous amethyst on the headset, and spokes encrusted with precious stones."

Even the egalitarian Paul de Vivie, who popularized cycle-touring in France, belonged to a club closed to working men. A bicycle at the end of the nineteenth century cost nearly 60 times what a worker earned in a day. But this was just the constituency that defected to the car. Cars went faster, without sweat, and they beat even a gold-plated bike as a sign of conspicuous consumption. The men who put their money behind *L'Auto* were placed to realize it. The Baron de Zuylen de Nyevelt de Haart, a prosperous Dutchman, never deigned to drive a car, preferring a horse and carriage, but he did create the *Automobile-Club de France*. Gustave Adolphe Clément made bicycles but moved to cars and airships. Clément Bayard and Édouard Michelin could sell more and bigger tires to drivers than cyclists. Alexandre Darracq was happy to back anybody, even the opposition, if it sold more cars.

There were two more curious backers. One was the Viscount de Montureux—probably François Armand Eugène Caillot de Montureux—who got the idea that cars on legs would be better than cars on wheels. The other was the boss of the Française bicycle company, John Varmm Hammond. He and Desgrange became friends—and Desgrange and the first Tour would suffer because of it.

All were businessmen first, politicians second and sports fans third. They wanted a profit and they wanted Desgrange to keep his opinions to himself. The second was easier than the first. Desgrange had to publicize his paper. He couldn't advertise in other papers. There was no radio, no television. The only place he could boast of his paper was in his own paper.

Giffard had that problem as well. He resolved it by organizing ever larger sports events. He promoted the first Paris marathon. He helped start Paris–Roubaix. Why? Because a newspaper could build excitement around men who raced from one city to another in an era when few had been beyond their village. The wish to know more could be satisfied only by buying next day's paper in which, with luck, would be news of more thrilling events to come.

Desgrange could do no more than copy. If there was a popular race, he duplicated it or ran a longer one. He avoided politics but he took to nagging. Jacques Goddet, who succeeded him, said: "He wanted *L'Auto* to be the premier journal of French society… There was no crime in its pages, no obscenity (the word 'pornography' wasn't yet common), but a vigorous campaign against syphilis, a taboo subject, against the ravages of this silent shame which, by being hidden, was spreading still further. There were editorials in favor of hygiene, of cleanliness."

Desgrange told the French they were weedy, that too few had been strong or nourished enough to fight the Franco-Prussian war. France had lost Alsace to the occupiers and seen its capital besieged. Desgrange was ashamed of France and its people. They should exercise more, he insisted. And they should lay off sex. He preached that "a cyclist in training has no more use for a woman than for the previous day's socks."

His paper appeared on its yellow paper on October 16, 1900, four pages for five centimes. The first three pages were sport and the fourth advertising. High among the advertisers were de Dion ("small cars, petrol-engined tricycles and quadricycles") and Clément, who boasted that his salesman in Spain "has just accomplished, given the nature of the roads, a true *tour de force* in driving from Paris to Madrid in his little Clément car." There was interest but readers weren't thrilled. Circulation stuck at 20,000. *Le Vélo* sold four times as many. The accountants said they needed 25,000 to make ends meet. And investors said they needed still more to make money. Desgrange's tenure looked risky.

He was saved by his rugby-and-cycling-and-motoring writer. Géo Lefèvre—he died in 1961 and you'll find him in the cemetery of Sompuis in the Marne region—was 26. He was a champion of the *Stade Français* cycling club in Paris, fancied his talent as a writer and asked Giffard for a job. Desgrange admired what he wrote and poached him. He was one of the few people in *L'Auto*'s board room next to the stone staircase on the second floor at 10 rue du Faubourg Montmartre on November 20, 1902. The floors above were occupied by a dubious photographer, a workshop that supplied flowers and feathers for women's hats, and a handful of private apartments.

"What we need is something to nail Giffard's beak shut," Desgrange said at this crisis meeting. But what? He looked at the second man present, Georges Prade, then at Lefèvre. The young cyclist, needing to say something, blurted: "Let's organize a race that lasts several days, longer than anything else. Like the six-days on the track but on the road." Desgrange, Lefèvre recalled, hesitated before answering: "If I

understand you right, *petit Géo*, you're proposing a Tour de France."
The name wasn't new. One of the most popular books in France, *Le Tour de la France par Deux Enfants*, appeared in 1877. A "tour de France" was what apprentices made to win experience. It was, though, the first time it had been used in cycling.

The idea intrigued Desgrange but he was uncertain. "You want to kill Maurice Garin and his like?" he asked. He looked at his watch, announced it time for lunch, and invited Lefèvre to join him. They left the office, turned left and walked to the junction with the boulevard

The display is modest, the significance enormous—for it was here that Géo Lefèvre explained his "Tour de France" to Henri Desgrange.

Montmartre. This isn't, by the way, the famous Montmartre, the hill of artists and poets. It's the less distinguished lower Montmartre of, said the historian Jacques Seray, "a thousand occupations, of industry, of business and of pleasure."

At the top of the road they turned right to a brasserie at number eight. There is confusion about what it was called. Some say the Taverne Zimmer, others the Café de Madrid. Whatever its name, it's still there—now called TGI Friday—and an old bike and a handful of photos and advertisements mark the occasion. Inviting Lefèvre to lunch was significant, said Jacques Goddet. "It was a rare gesture which eloquently demonstrated the shock [of the Tour idea] suffered by a man extremely rigorous about expenses."

Desgrange and Lefèvre ate well but spoke little. Only when their espresso arrived did Desgrange say: "Explain this idea of yours." Lefèvre ran through it, making up most as he went, outlining a race so colossal that nobody could exceed it—to a Frenchman the boundaries of France were the limits of the known world, or at any rate the world worth knowing—and taking in so many towns and villages that papers would sell everywhere.

"And the cost?" Desgrange asked.

"The towns will welcome the publicity," Lefèvre hazarded. "They may pay the costs for us."

Desgrange hesitated again. He never did anything without Victor Goddet's approval. "He needs to be convinced," he told Lefèvre, not sure he would be, maybe hoping he wouldn't. The two walked back the way they'd come. Jacques Goddet recalled: "The Goddet in question, my father, had full control over expenses and what they went on. He listened attentively to the plan that the two accomplices explained to him and, without hesitating, to their deep surprise, handed them the keys to the safe (which never left him) and said simply: 'Take whatever you need.'"

Part Two: Départ Réel

The opening truce, or rolling start, lasts as long as it needs to. The riders pedal smartly but they don't race. The flag then drops for the second time as the race starts properly, the "départ réel".

1

You Go Instead, Petit Géo…

You can imagine investors listening to Desgrange explain this wild and expensive race. There was their paper losing money and here was Desgrange planning to spend more. Imagine, too, the despair when the post brought just a trickle of entries. The race went too far. It lasted too long. There was too much risk of coming home without a sou. And Paris wasn't going to hear of it. There'd be no hooligan cycle-racing in the city, ruled the *préfet-de-police*, Louis Lépine. Imagine the heaviness of heart that went with rejigging the route, shortening distances, spending money on paying riders to take part.

Desgrange had driven the route several times and, with the date still far off, he felt confident all was in place. But nearer the day he lost his nerve. He became a general leading from the rear. A long way in the rear because he didn't even go to the start. That was left to Lefèvre, who'd been told to follow the race by train and bike, and *L'Auto's* general secretary Georges Abran, a florid gent whose tedious humor included calling people by their wrong name. Dressed in a general's uniform, his job was to wave the riders away and spend the rest of the day traveling and in restaurants. Arrangements at the finish were left to regional reporters.

Denied the right to bring his race into Paris, Desgrange had to start and finish outside. Nobody knows why he chose Montgeron for the start. Ville d'Abray for the finish is easier because it is the last town in Seine-et-Oise before crossing into the *département* of the Seine, where Lépine and his ban held sway. The race ended at 147 rue de Versailles, outside the Père Vélo restaurant, renamed Père Auto to honor the race. François Mitterand used to lunch there, at a table near the fireplace, before he became president. It's now Il Boccaccio, an Italian restaurant.

Desgrange had been to Montgeron because other races were held there. He knew the family that owned the Réveil Matin on the junction of the roads to Melun and Corbeil because he'd lunched there. It had a reputation for honest, inexpensive meals and it welcomed cyclists, which wasn't always the case. If he had a sense of history, he'd have known it had been a coaching inn and that two drivers were murdered there in the hope they were carrying gold.

The crowd was good but not enormous that first day of July, 1903. Street singers and mandolin players touted for coins and an Algerian known as Boum-Boum sold Coco, the drink of the day, from a tank on his back. The first to sign on were Ellinamour—of whom no more is known than that his first name started with H—and Léon Pernette, the last Claude Chapperon and Émile Moulin, who'd missed their train and had to ride from Paris.

The riders, a random collection were they not all male, went into the bar's cellars to change. Among them was Garin, smuggled out of Italy as a child and taken to the very north of France, to Roubaix and then to Lens, a coal-mining town where he was safe from Italian justice. Desgrange called him "the chimney sweep", because that's what Garin had been and because he gave nicknames to all the riders to make them more interesting. Garin was also "the little bulldog". Others were known as "the florist" and even "the heel-pedaler."

There too was the village blacksmith from Grisolles, south of Montauban, near Toulouse. He had "thighs and calves like the pillars of a cathedral", according to L'Auto. And a blond mustache. The day he went to buy a bike, the man at the shop said he ought to ride this new Tour de France he'd heard about. Nobody in Jean Dargassies' family had ever left the surroundings of Grisolles, a village which led a blameless life making brooms. He entered, though, and when he got no reply he made the journey of his life, north to Paris. There he walked shyly into L'Auto's office and said:

"Monsieur Lefèvre, I've come to ask you about the Tour de France."

We know that's what he said because Lefèvre was so tickled by this hick and his twanging southern accent that he told the tale verbatim.

"But look, you're already entered; you're on the list."

"Well, yes, I know but I wanted to know what to do next."

"It's all been published in detail in L'Auto."

"L'Auto... I don't think anyone reads that in Monnetaubanne."

Lefèvre reveled in reproducing Dargassies' pronounce-every-letter accent.

"Where?"

"Monnetaubanne, Tarn-et-Garonne."

"Oh, Montauban!"

"Yes. In the village of Grisolles. I didn't see *L'Auto*. The man who sold me my bike told me there was a Tour de France race and he said: 'Dargaties, you're made for that.'"

Dargaties was his real name. Lefèvre, like any self-respecting journalist, got it wrong. From then on, Dargaties became Jean Dargassies.

"Tell me," Lefèvre said, "have you ever actually ridden a cycle race?"

"No, but I've ridden from Grisolles to Montauban and back and I didn't even have to try. I'm a blacksmith; I'm not worried about tiredness."

The time limit for entries was 5pm on June 15, two weeks before the race. All Desgrange asked was a name, an address, the number of a rider's license, and ten francs for the whole race, five francs for a stage, and two francs for the thirteen amateurs who wanted to ride the Toulouse–Bordeaux part. If there weren't enough left by the last day of racing, Desgrange would enroll extras to make a show. And a show he needed because from the formal finish in Ville d'Abray there'd be a procession to the *Parc des Princes* and a sprint round the track. Desgrange wasn't going to be able to sell tickets if only two or three riders struggled to the end.

He also warned against tricks: "We plan to exercise an extraordinarily rigorous surveillance, especially at night, to enforce the rule banning pacemakers and *soigneurs*. We have already adopted three forms of surveillance—which we are keeping secret—which we know will guarantee the best results. And more than that, we've received a great many offers from friends in the areas the race crosses to keep a secret eye on the race."

This speaks of resolution but hints at pessimism. A man sure his race will go well sees no need to print repeated cautions in his newspaper. Desgrange wasn't convinced his head would be off the block before the blade fell. And for all the commotion at *L'Auto*'s office on the eve of the race, however unmissable the Tour de France, Desgrange backed out of making it the lead in that day's paper. The Tour started next day but Desgrange preferred the Gordon Bennett Cup car race another two days off. And which was in Ireland rather than France.

Next day Abran blew on his fingers at 1:30pm to call the riders. The Dutch author Jean Nelissen wrote of "men with big caps on their head and impressive mustaches, dressed in long, black pants and jerseys with long sleeves, placed their race bikes against the wall to go into the changing room to sign the starting list in front of an impressive man with an enormous white mustache, dressed in a general's uniform: Monsieur Abran."

The comic-opera general walked 600 metres from the café, towards Draveil, and called the riders to follow. He reminded them they weren't to stop at bars or hotels along the way, that unlike other races they weren't to have pacers. And then at 3:16pm he either dropped his yellow flag or fired his revolver—nobody agrees which—and retired to the bar to write of how "the men waved their hats, the ladies their umbrellas. One felt they would have liked to touch the steel muscles of the most courageous champions since antiquity. Yes, the most courageous because—a revolution in our splendid sport of cycling—the race will be run without pacemakers. An end to the combines and to ruffians of every stamp. Only muscles and energy will win glory and fortune. Who will carry off the first prize, entering the pantheon where only supermen may go? I do not hesitate to make Maurice Garin, the white bulldog, my favorite."

Why "the white bulldog"? Who knows…

There were stars, like Garin and the chunky German, Josef Fischer, and the wrestler figure of Hippolyte Aucouturier, his mustache wider than his cheeks, his jersey vivid red and blue. And the rest were largely also-rans, unknowns and simple adventurers like Dargassies. Most wore what they wore to work. Some had shorts. Almost all had canvas bags for food, tools, their route sheet and a card to present along the way to show they had followed the course.

Desgrange saw nothing but didn't lack imagination. Our men, he waxed, are going to race "madly, unflaggingly from Marseille to Bordeaux, passing along the roseate and dreaming fields sleeping under the sun, across the calm fields of the Vendée, following the Loire which flows on still and silent."

He was right about "madly." The field cracked on at 35 kilometres per hour, which is more than everyday riders manage even now, and by 11pm Garin and Émile Pagie were at Nevers. They were preceded by Fernand Mercier, who arranged the finishes, and followed by Lefèvre, his bags full of lists and numbers and train timetables.

"No car for me, just my bike," Lefèvre remembered. "I was 26 years old and I followed the riders as far as the nearest station where the timetable would let me catch an express that would get me to the finish before the riders. Or I would take the train before the riders started to be able to surprise them on the road during the night. Having checked the riders, I had to tag on to the group or to the leaders, whom I needed to watch particularly carefully, then take the train from a big station which would allow me to jump into an express or a fast train and get to the stage town before the riders. After every stage, I had to write enough words to fill a page of *L'Auto*, transmit my story to the paper, and only then was I allowed to eat and get a few hours' sleep."

He went by train, he said, "because at that time Desgrange had no confidence in cars." Which is odd, given the name of his journal and the nature of his backers. On the first day, he didn't make it. The riders reached the quai de Vaise in Lyon around nine in the morning, heralded by trumpeters. They'd ridden 476 kilometres in eighteen hours. Lefèvre, with a train, took longer and got to the line in time to find Garin having a drink. Making the best of his blunder, he cabled: "They are riding faster than the train!" He could also have mentioned that nobody was there to see them: there'd been no way to warn spectators that the race was running early.

Garin won the first stage in the impressively precise 17 hours, 45 minutes, 13.2 seconds (impressively precise not least because Lefèvre, the timekeeper, got there after the riders). Aucouturier won the next two stages and held a handsome lead by Toulouse, where all that remains of the vélodrome on which the day finished are trees at the entrance to a rugby pitch. But then he faded, saying a spectator had given him lemonade mixed with acid. Garin held steady, made up the loss and won the Tour—with the cheating help of the Tour de France. And why did officials cheat, handing food to him though it was against the rules? Because Garin was sponsored by La Française. And the boss of La Française was Desgrange's chum and an investor in the paper.

Garin won more than enough to set himself up in business in Lens—his filling station is still there but not as it was—and the town turned out to meet him. He said: "The 2,500 kilometres that I've just ridden seem a long line, gray and monotonous, where nothing stood out from anything else. I suffered on the road; I was hungry, I was thirsty, I was sleepy, I suffered, I cried between Lyon and Marseille. I see myself, from the start of the Tour de France, like a bull pierced by *banderillas*, who pulls the *banderillas* with him, never able to rid himself of them." He didn't, you notice, mention sporting aberrations such as handing a spectator 100 francs not to lend a bike to a rival. Nor the broken bottles scattered on the road by the leaders to delay their chasers.

And Dargassies, the shambling, innocent who knew what tiredness meant? What of him? Well, he wasn't deterred by the stars, of whom—not reading *L'Auto*—he'd probably never heard anyway. On the fourth day there were just 30 in the race. Dargassies left Toulouse and headed the race through his village. "The whole of Grisolles is by the side of the road," Lefèvre reported. "They're here to see Dargassies, the champion of the region." The rest slowed to give him his glory. It started the tradition of allowing local heroes their moment and it established Dargassies as the first "regional" of the Tour. "When he rode by," *L'Auto* wrote, "every voice shouted in encouragement, in a long avenue of people all the way to Montauban."

That day he once more passed through "Monnetaubanne" and on into Moissac. The control was in the Hôtel du Luxembourg. Dargassies was three minutes behind the leaders and his front fork was broken. It's always Eugène Christophe and his broken fork that you read about but Dargassies was first. And being a blacksmith, he found a smithy and made a repair.

In Paris he finished thirteen hours behind Garin. His eleventh place won 145 francs. When he reached Grisolles he sent a telegram to Lefèvre: "Got back home today. All my compatriots are crazy, crazier than me. Everybody at the station, music, flowers, speech. Fame! Fame!" He left his family forge—you can still find it today, although much changed—and opened a bike shop in the village, on a corner of the rue de Lumel. He lies in Grisolles still, in the cemetery. But there's a better yarn still to come…

2

Who Are You, Henri Desgrange?

We are shaped by our era. Henri Desgrange was born in 1865. He was five when France and Germany went to war. Again. Napoleon had toured western Europe, snaffling all he wanted. Now the wheel was turning. Napoleon was in Elba, exiled after Waterloo. France had lost Waterloo after German troops reinforced the struggling British. And now France and Germany were at war again.

The fighting spread across northern France for five months and ended with Paris being besieged and finally falling at the start of 1871. Desgrange remembered it well, not least because the Germans decided to starve the city to death or force its surrender during a long, cold winter. Parisians ate cats, dogs, rats and even the city's two circus elephants. Finally the Germans bombarded Paris with heavy cannon and the French surrendered.

Desgrange saw the suffering and destruction. He went to school, to the Collège Rollin—it's still in the avénue Trudaine in the ninth arrondissement, although it's now the Lycée Jacques-Decour—and mastered his baccalaureate and then a law license. He married, had a daughter, and then divorced. Neither woman appeared again in his public life. He had shares in the *Parc des Princes* and other venues, notably the *Vélodrome d'Hiver* indoor track near the Eiffel Tower, and he invested in property.

No nation is less than embarrassed when vanquished. Adults are angry and children resentful. Desgrange was resentful. France was going through liberalization. It wasn't to the liking of the old guard, of industrialists and the church, who saw the country going to the dogs. Desgrange leaned the same way. Had he not, were he not an *anti-Dreyfusard*, his backers would never have employed him.

Gautier Demouveaux, in his history at the University of Lyon 2, says: "In the editorial of the first issue of *L'Auto*, Henri Desgrange said again that there would be no politics in his paper. But his idea of the Tour de France came from an ideology not at all neutral. Because, for all that the race was created to eliminate the competition from *Le Vélo*, Desgrange didn't hide its moralizing aspect. The Tour was inspired by nationalism and the ideas of Maurice Barrès, anchored to the political right. Desgrange never hid his friendship with Barrès [Barrès was a leader of the anti-Dreyfus movement, wrote anti-Semitic pamphlets, and believed in racial supremacy based on his reading of the Bible] and offered him a column in his paper."

On the other hand, while Barrès said Dreyfus was guilty simply because he was Jewish, there's no sign of anti-Semitism in Desgrange. Where they agreed was that France had failed because its men weren't up to it. Evidence: the army had rejected thousands of recruits as unfit or unwell. Physical and mental degeneration—"the country is going to the dogs and young people are to blame"—was a popular idea on the right and a credo of the élite. Desgrange's opening editorial was a call for stiffening of sinews.

"We live better and we live faster than before," Desgrange wrote. "The generations before ours went through the lack of curiosity of college life, the never-ending walking round the school yard, the endless studies when the soul yearned to be outdoors; then, liberated, the monotony of daily work…life without end, always the same, the same marriage, the same children, the same imposing stomach of the head clerk at work…

"But now our little French kids go to a college where, almost everywhere, there's a sports club which takes them, shapes them, teaches them to defend themselves, to attack everywhere. Whether it's soccer or running, they become fighters, with the need to win, feeling the humiliation of defeat, the spirit of solidarity in teams. They acquire temperament, decisiveness, judgment, courage, initiative. And out of college they are armed for the battle, not hiding behind their mothers' skirts, ready to make their own way, go where they must, even far away, even to the colonies.

"And soon our race will find itself radically transformed. Like the Anglo-Saxon race, it will extend everywhere when our children have learned in their daily sports battles how to solve their problems, to fight for themselves…And then we'll see the French have children, lots of children in their own image, who will have, like English children, teeth that can bite and the firm will to succeed."

Jacques Goddet said "Desgrange imposed on himself a life of submitting himself to daily physical exercise. It had to demand, according to his draconian theories, a violent effort, prolonged, repeated, sometimes going as far as pain, demanding tenacity and even a certain stoicism. He took on a crusade against Original Inertia, against the soften-

Henri Desgrange never stopped competing, even in his dying days challenging himself to hobble faster across his bedroom floor.

ing of the body in the face of a society keen to suppress physical effort. He appointed himself the apostle of the fight to safeguard character. Suffer and sweat! And that meant a permanent individual culture of cross-country, at least three times a week, in the *parc de St-Cloud*. Nor did he hold back: he ran for at least an hour, never missing out Jardies hill, the fierce slope in the center of the park used by hardened runners."

When you know that, a lot falls into place. It explains why the Tour went around the borders, because it reinforced those borders and national pride within them. Schools did not teach the geography of

France. Few people in France, say Jean-Luc Boeuf and Yves Léonard in *La République du Tour de France*, knew the shape of their country. Maps weren't pinned to walls. When Desgrange outlined France in *L'Auto* to show where his race would go, it was the first time most people realized their country was a hexagon.

Desgrange wasn't just spiking a rival. He was creating pride. His Tour was the extreme test, to show men could rise to challenges. His ideal course would be one that only one could finish. He would be a superman and yet he would be human, an example. And, for the moment anyway, he would be French.

Superman wasn't the creation of DC Comics. Goliath was a superman. He came to a sticky end, it's true, but that he was felled by the boyish David shows, like Peter Pan vanquishing Captain Hook, that we can all aspire to greatness, that no challenge is too great.

Desgrange's era was of races of staggering length, from Paris to Brest and back or from Bordeaux to Paris. They took a long time and then the racers rested. The Tour strung these races end to end. There would be rest days but not rest weeks. The roads were bad, the distances so great, the challenge so appalling, that some stages began one day and finished the next, riding through the night. The shortest in the first Tour was 268 kilometres, from Toulouse to Bordeaux. And it was that short only because, just once, Desgrange hesitated over what a human could do. He'd wanted to go from Marseille to Bordeaux without the break in Toulouse. How far? 691 kilometres.

The demands were dreadful. Josef Fischer, the size of a wrestler, "collapsed on a chair, crying, his tears cutting pink channels through the dust of his face."

"I've never felt like this. My head, that's fine. My legs are good. But I'm just not advancing. It's my stomach."

"Your stomach?"

"Yes…It's over…It's over."

"*Allons, allons*! Eat something and you'll feel better."

"He eats, he gets up, clenches his hands, gently takes his bike. Poor vanquished champion!"

It did him no good. He abandoned 135 kilometres from the finish.

As soon as he realized that first Tour would be a success, Desgrange went to be there, catching the train to Toulouse. The shareholders were delighted, too, because their 20,000 copies a day had returned in July to the 60,000 they had been at the start and then risen to 65,000 and even peaks of 100,000. Pierre Giffard, who had initially given only a short paragraph to the Tour, admitted that "the success and the fame of the Tour are as great as its importance."

It was the end for his paper, though. *Le Vélo* lasted another year, until November 1904. Other rivals, *Le Monde Sportif* and *Les Sports*, also gave up. Giffard went off to report the Russo-Japanese war but, so far as cycling was concerned, his beak was nailed shut. There was no rancor, however. De Dion, whose idea it had been to sink him, insisted Desgrange employ him at *L'Auto*.

They probably danced all night in the Faubourg Montmartre. The riders doubtless less, because they were tired. But fourteen of the twenty-one finishers won prizes and the rest had at least their daily start fee. Desgrange was delighted—but a year later he wanted to walk away in disgust. He was a victim of his success. He could warn about this army of referees patrolling the course but the night was dark and the riders spaced. They laughed at Lefèvre, telling him a young boy should be home in bed.

It was inevitable that complaint and protest would arrive. Belgians said officials had snubbed their riders to favor the French; friends of Aucouturier insisted his stomach trouble was from a poisoned drink and friends of Garin protested in turn about Aucouturier. But that was nothing...

Garin is buried with others of his family in the Cimetière Est, off the rue Constant Darras in the suburb of Sallaumines. He spent his last days in confusion, wandering into the police station asking "Where's the control? Where's the control?" before being led home.

There's not much to commend the area unless you're a war buff. The battlefield of Vimy Ridge and its Canadian memorial is just to the north, where 12,000 died taking the ridge of Nôtre Dame de Lorette in 1917. On the hill is the French national cemetery filled from battles in 1914 and 1915. Among the 22,970 bodies, many unidentified, is François Faber, the "giant of Colombes", who in 1909 rode through knee-deep puddles and a mountain gale that twice blew him off his bike, survived being kicked by a horse, and ran a kilometre to the finish with a bike that no longer had a chain. He took all five stages between Roubaix and Nice and won again in Bordeaux.

The Tour's first foreign winner is buried there because he was shot while carrying an injured colleague across no man's land. There is a plaque in the giant basilica. There is, though, no memorial in France to Maurice Garin. It was years before the gravediggers at Sallaumines knew whose grave they had diligently cleared of leaves, along with all the others in their charge. They knew nothing until an Italian television crew began filming there. The little chimney sweep's name is not listed on the stone.

Jean-Marie Jasniewicz, the senior attendant, is the son of an immigrant from Poland. Poles came for a better life, thousands working in the mines. Among them, Edward Stablewski, who as Jean Stablinski won the world and French championship and rode the Tour.

Legend says Garin came to France after being exchanged for a round of cheese. So far as the truth can be found, it's likely the family wanted to leave Italy but couldn't afford complicated emigration applications which stood every chance of being declined. The cheese was probably all the family could pay a guide to lead Garin over the mountains.

Maybe that common background led Jasniewicz and his assistant, Maurice Vernaldé, to take Garin to their heart. "Our politicians, they have no culture," Vernaldé complained. "If Garin had been a soccer star or a wartime hero, we'd have a statue or a plaque. But nobody cares about the winner of the first Tour de France."

It could be because he cheated. Nobody's sure but the accusations may include expanding cycle-racing to taking a train. That was certainly what Lucien Pothier did. Garin was surely guilty of taking short cuts and hanging on to cars. Pierre Chevallier doubtless did the same because he was repeatedly left for dead in the darkness only to pop back fresher than he should have been. If he didn't actually ride in a car then he used the popular wheeze of tying a wire to a car and the other end to a cork between his teeth. From a distance it looked as though he was grimacing from effort and at night the wire was invisible.

Garin had so many crashes and punctures that rumor grew the others were trying to put him out of the race. And well they might because Garin was again using his Française connections and Lefèvre's innocence to have food handed to him. The last thing Lefèvre felt able to tell his boss was that the previous year's winner had dropped out because he was hungry.

Spectators, too, became enflamed. They let their favorites pass and then felled trees across the road. Word reached the bike-making city of St-Étienne that Garin had received extra food at the expense of the local favorite, Antoine Fauré. Fauré's fans waited on the col de la République which drops into the town and began beating up Garin and an Italian, Giovanni Gerbi, whose broken fingers forced him to drop out. Lefèvre scared off the rioters with gun shots. Next day the crowd returned to beat up the officials.

Desgrange fined Garin 500 francs for the illegal food and after that the race quieted down. The *Union Vélocipèdique Française* kept quiet until the fuss had died. Then in November it waded in with nine disqualifications and bans. Desgrange was furious, insisting he had already punished the riders and that the UVF was trespassing. It wouldn't be the last time that Tour organizers saw themselves above the sport's governors.

"The Tour de France is finished," Desgrange wailed, "and the second edition will, I fear, also be the last. It has died of its success, of the blind passions that it unleashed, the abuse and dirty suspicions…We will therefore leave it to others to take the chance of taking on an adventure on the scale of the Tour de France."

Bluff? Or the emotion of a man who hadn't had time to reflect? Perhaps both. Looking back, there was little chance Desgrange wanted to abandon the Tour and still less that his shareholders would let him. The Tour had saved the paper. Without the Tour, even without opposition, *L'Auto* was a snuffed candle.

3

A Stern Father

Desgrange called himself, or at any rate never objected to being called, *le père du Tour*, the father of the Tour. Nonsense, of course, because the race hadn't been his idea, he refused to put it on his front page the day before it started, he refused to be at the start, and he traveled to Toulouse to be with it only when it was a sure success. The *père du Tour* was Géo Lefèvre. It was his idea, and it was he who rode his bike to follow it. But legends are created by hiding the bodies and Desgrange pushed Lefèvre off cycling and on to rugby reporting.

The main climb of 1903, the col de la République, was one that enthusiasts did regularly. Among them was a stumpy, opinionated man called Paul de Vivie, who wrote in his cycling magazine as Vélocio. It was de Vivie, you'll remember, who belonged to a club that excluded working men. De Vivie himself was a silk merchant.

De Vivie called the République by its other name, the col du Grand Bois (Big Wood Pass), which suggest pro-monarchy, anti-republican leanings which Desgrange's contemporaries wouldn't have found strange. De Vivie imported bikes from England but found their gears too high. He was passed on a keep-fit ride up the mountain by one of his own readers—puffing a pipe. Offended, de Vivie invented derailleur gears.

Desgrange was against gears. He sought the Ultimate Athlete; the bike was a necessity that got in the way. The Touring Club de France organized a challenge in 1902 in which an amateur with a three-speed derailleur beat a professional without one over 200 kilometres of hills. Desgrange wrote: "I applaud this test, but I still feel that variable gears are only for people over 45. Isn't it better to triumph by the strength of your muscles than by the artifice of a derailleur? We are getting soft. Come on fellows. Let's say that the test was a fine demonstration—for our grandparents! As for me, give me a fixed gear!"

The fixed gear was what made mountains intimidating. All riders had was a choice of sprockets, one larger than the other, one on each side of the back wheel. They became adept at turning their wheel and riding off again. The devious, when they knew the hill, tricked the less knowledgeable by spinning their wheel twice, staying on the original gear and bluffing rivals into using a gear too high or too low.

In 1905 Desgrange included the Ballon d'Alsace in the northeast, near Mulhouse. The Ballon was a real mountain, at 1,247 metres only slightly higher than the République but quite different. It rained a lot, the wind blew and for much of the year snow made it impassable. At the top, now, is a memorial to René Pottier. Desgrange boasted nobody could ride this monster. So imagine what wasn't his surprise, as the French say, when Pottier not only rode all the way but, the following year, overtook Desgrange's car. Pottier won four consecutive stages through the Alps and the Vosges in 1906. He took an hour's lead on the day from Grenoble and had the arrogance to wait at a bar with a jug of wine until the others caught up, then to join them and beat them into Nice by 26 minutes.

He was cycling's first star climber. His lark with the wine suggests a joker. He was anything but. He was driven by demons, rarely smiled, hardly spoke. His large eyes were perpetually sad, his mouth below a wide mustache always turned down. On January 25, 1907, he was found hanging from a hook at the Peugeot headquarters in Levallois-Perret, a northwestern suburb of Paris. There was no note but his brother said he had died "of sentimental reasons", which many thought meant his wife had left him during the Tour.

Desgrange was torn between excess and fear. The news from Levallois-Perret couldn't have reassured him. But it did nothing but encourage Alphonse Steinès.

Alphonse Steinès is the Great Unknown who created the modern Tour—at the cost of almost dying in the process. He was born in Luxembourg and described himself as "an eternal cycle-tourist." He believed the Tour should go over not just the relatively mild Vosges but the steeper and longer Pyrenees along the Spanish border. Until then the Tour had stayed on the almost flat roads of the Garonne valley to the north. The only roads across the Pyrenees were tracks. They didn't need to be more: people didn't cross the mountains because there were no roads and there were no roads because there was no demand.

None of this deterred Steinès. In late middle age he was a jovial-looking, round-faced man with circular spectacles and an air of good living. His appearance confirms his reputation as a man who enjoyed needling Desgrange, forever pushing him to be braver, more outrageous. We know the conversation that ensued and the drama that followed it because Steinès recounted it.

"*Patron*," he remembered saying, "I'll give you a plan to make the Tour still bigger this year."

"Bigger? You think it's not big enough already?"

"No. We've got to touch all the frontiers."

"Frontiers...frontiers...Your idea of going to Metz four years ago wasn't exactly brilliant."

"How do you mean? Not brilliant?"

"The German government ended up by banning it...No, Steinès, the mistake is in not staying strictly in France."

"Ah, there *patron*, I don't agree. You know very well that all our neighbors want us to visit them."

"I know. But it's not always easy. How about Spain?" Desgrange was thinking of the Pyrenees. It's impossible to get to Spain or to edge the border without crossing them.

"Exactly," Steinès beamed. "Spain! I think we'd be able to cross the Pyrenees."

"The Pyrenees? You're joking."

Steinès wasn't joking and he argued so long that Desgrange crumbled. But not before Desgrange exploded: "You want me to kill them!"

Steinès diverted the stage from Nîmes to Toulouse to Perpignan instead. Going there through Luchon and Bayonne took race over the cols de Peyresourde, Aspin, Tourmalet and Aubisque.

"How can you dare to say it'd be a success," Desgrange exploded. "You're going through places that don't exist."

"What doesn't exist?"

"What I mean...that they don't exist. To climb as far as your cols, there isn't even a road."

"No road? What do you know about it?"

Steinès knew the area. He had ridden a bike and driven a car there. Desgrange grew angrier and, to get rid of him, told him to look for himself. Steinès went to Pau. He called on a man called Blanchet, the engineer of bridges and roads. Blanchet listened amazed. He said the staff of *L'Auto* must have gone mad to consider the Aubisque. *L'Auto*, of course, hadn't considered the Aubisque at all. Only Steinès had considered it.

"Do you *know* the Aubisque?" Blanchet asked.

"Of course," said Steinès airily. "I've just been up there. It's obvious that in the state it's in now, the Tour couldn't go up there. But you're going to arrange it."

"Me? But I haven't got a penny for that."

"No money? Shame. Ah well, too bad, I'll get you what you think necessary. How much do you think it would cost?"

Blanchet guessed 5,000 francs. It was much more than Steinès imagined. He called Desgrange. He motioned to Blanchet to pick up the extension and together they heard him gasp: "Five thousand francs? But you're mad! You want to ruin us? I'll give you 1,500, not a centime more."

"Excellent," said Steinès. "Did you say 2,000?" Blanchet insisted over dinner that the job couldn't be done for less than 5,000. Steinès winked and said he'd find the rest "in an old drawer somewhere."

That left the Tourmalet, loftier than the Aubisque and the highest Pyrenean pass on the French side of the mountains. Steinès couldn't cross it so early in the year so he returned to Paris and came back a month before the Tour. He went into Sainte-Marie-de-Campan, where years later Eugène Christophe mended his forks on the village forge. There he ate at the inn opposite the church and the landlady found a driver called Dupont from nearby Bagnères-de-Bigorre. Local knowledge would be essential.

The Tourmalet is nineteen kilometres long, straight from the middle of the village in a series of hard and then easier slopes before a beak of a twist roughly where the ski resort of La Mongie stands now. Just after there, Dupont's car stuck in the snow. He and Steinès started to walk, but Dupont turned back after 600 metres.

"Bears come over from Spain when it snows," he shouted. "It's six o'clock. It'll be dark soon. I'm not going any further." If Steinès was stupid enough to press on then he could do it alone. Dupont told him to look out for four-metre poles stuck in the snow in the middle of the track.

"Wait for me in Barèges," Steinès called back, referring to the far side of the mountain where the river Bastan bursts through the village at its foot.

"I will," said Dupont, "but it's a long way, here to Barèges by foot. Ten or twelve kilometres." And he reversed and disappeared. Steinès grasped his stick and set off into the snow. He soon felt less confident. He heard voices. Who would wait on a mountain for travelers by night, and why? It turned out to be youngsters watching sheep with their dog. Steinès called to one.

"Son, do you know the Tourmalet well?"

"Certainly."

"Could you guide me?"

"Well…"

"I'll give you twenty francs and a gold coin. When we get to the other top, I'll give you another one."

"I don't need money."

"Everyone needs money."

"No, I don't. But I'll take you anyway."

The two kilometres to the summit took two and a half hours. Night fell without stars. Clouds blocked the moon. The boy insisted on going back to his sheep, expecting a beating if he didn't. He disappeared and Steinès rested on a rock. He considered sitting there until dawn, then realized he'd freeze before he saw it. He slipped on the icy road. And then he fell, tumbling into a stream, wet now as well as cold. He climbed back to the road and again fell in the snow. He sat and cried. Then he pressed on, blind in the shadow of the mountain. Exhausted now and stumbling, he heard another voice. A challenge.

"Who's that?"

Steinès didn't answer.

"Tell me who goes there or I'll shoot."

"I'm a lost traveler. I've just come across the Tourmalet."

"Oh, it's you, Monsieur Steinès! We were expecting you!"

"How do you mean?"

"We got a phone call at Sainte-Marie-de-Campan. Everybody's at Barèges. It's coming on for three o'clock. There are search teams of guides out looking for you." Barèges was awake with its lights on. L'Auto's correspondent was there, a man called Lanne-Camy.

"My dear Steinès, what a state you're in!" he said. He took him for a bath and new clothes, too large but welcome.

"I promised to telegram Desgrange," Steinès told Lanne-Camy.

"And what are you going to tell him?"

"I don't know yet. I've got to think about it. Have you got some paper?"

Lanne-Camy found some.

"Tell me, old chap. Is the road good at the top when the snow has melted?"

"The road? But it's just a mule track!"

Steinès hesitated.

"What are you going to wire?" Lanne-Camy asked.

"Je ne sais pas. Ah! Tant pis! A la grâce de Dieu..." ("I don't know. Oh, heck...may God save me...")

And he picked up the pencil.

"Henri Desgrange, *L'Auto*, Paris," he wrote. "Crossed Tourmalet stop. Very good road stop. Perfectly feasible."

4
You Are But Mere Babies

Christmas doesn't necessarily bring goodwill to all men. Nicolae Ceauşescu was shot on Christmas Day 1989. One of the lesser grievances against him was declaring all the bears in Romania his personal property and shooting them from helicopters. These days the bears live in peace, except for the few boxed up and shipped to the Pyrenees.

Bears in the mountains vanished years ago, which is why they're being reintroduced from Romania. But they were a reality when Steinès crossed the Tourmalet. Two dozen riders said they had no intention of riding. "It's murder!", Lucien Petit-Breton protested. "Those bastards want our skin!" And if it wasn't bears, it was the climb, the track, the thunder. "People were telling us about avalanches, roads collapsed, of the killer mountains and the Thunder of God!", recalled the stick-thin Parisian, Gustave Garrigou.

Once more Desgrange stayed at home, saying he was unwell. He sent Victor Breyer, instead. Breyer was another recruit from *Le Vélo*. He rose to be president of the *Union Cycliste Internationale* but for the moment he was Goddet's deputy. Breyer and a handful of other officials drove to the top of the Aubisque—cautiously because of the bad road, despite *L'Auto*'s expense, and because cars were prone to conk out in thin air.

They stopped at the top, stepped out, put on coats, looked around and checked their watches. The riders were late and the officials grew worried. Had the predictions come to pass? And then, struggling towards them, they saw a local rider, François Lafourcade. They ran to him. Where were the others? What had happened? Lafourcade, who like so many others died in the war, stared and rode on without speaking. The stage was 326 kilometres long, it had started at 3:30am, he had already ridden the Tourmalet, and he had had enough. He picked his way down the other side and waited for the rest.

Fifteen minutes later, Octave Lapize arrived. The lesser star, the man from nearby Lahonton, had ridden; "Curly" Lapize was walking. This was the world turned upside down. Lapize was also a great deal more upset, or perhaps just more daring at abusing officials. "*Vous êtes assassins! Oui, des assassins!*", he snarled. Whether you translate it as "assassins" or "killers" or "murderers", the sentiment is clear.

L'Auto wrote of drama and bravery. It was almost all made up because barely anyone but officials made it up there and riders were too far apart to follow. Desgrange was thrilled. It had worked and he wasn't going to cop any blame. Now he didn't need Steinès to convince him. The Tour would go into the still higher Alps.

"Oh Laffrey! Oh Bayard! Oh Tourmalet!", he whooped. "I don't hesitate to proclaim that compared to the Galibier you are but a pale and vulgar baby. In front of this giant there is nothing more for you to do but take off your hats and bow from down below." He had a way with words, that man. On the other hand, the Galibier was indeed 2,645 metres against the 2,116 of the Tourmalet. He was kind enough to urge riders "to redouble their prudence, all through the mountains, because horses, mules, donkeys, oxen, sheep, cows, goats, pigs, can all be wandering untethered on the road." The riders must have been grateful at the care he took to detail just which animals would send them flying over the handlebars.

Beside all this seriousness, there was room for fun and buccaneering. In the first years of the Tour there weren't enough riders to fill the card. If you fancied having a go, you sent in your entry and Desgrange would accept you. These privateers had various names but the most common was *touriste-routier*. Nothing was provided for them and nothing asked. At the end of each day they collected their suitcase from the train station, balanced it on their bars and rode round town until they found a cheap hotel. If they hadn't won enough to pay for one, they slept in barns or on benches. Some sang in the streets; at least one performed acrobatics and went round the crowd with a hat. Next day they put their bags back on the train and set off again on the Tour de France.

The most colorful *touriste-routier* was a policeman from the Mediterranean who rode the Tour as his vacation. Nothing pleased Jules Banino more than a challenge. The writer Roger Dries said of him:

"You saw him in all the sports events ever organized. There was a swimming meeting? He'd be the first to turn up, perched on his bike, and he'd dive into the sea and take part. A pole-climbing contest? Banino would be there. He once even took on the same wager as the Count of Monte Cristo, tying himself in a sack and being thrown into the Mediterranean at Tabau-Capeu. He almost drowned. He had to be pulled out in a hurry and he was hardly breathing when they got to him."

Banino was 51 when he rode the Tour in 1924 and nobody older has ever taken part. That summer was hot, and dust from unmade roads blinded him as the race cars passed. Eventually he finished outside the time limit and was thrown out. He set off to ride home to Nice. So too later that the night, did the Tour de France.

Stages rode through the night because there wasn't enough daylight to complete the distance. The custom was to ride in a group, nobody attacking, everybody profiting from the weak light thrown by following cars. Except that obviously someone *had* attacked because back came reports of a lone rider ahead. And going well. The stars looked to see who was missing. Everybody who mattered was there. The escapee must be a lesser-light. He was going to be taught a lesson. The peloton stepped up to 35 kilometres per hour on the rutted roads and plunged downhill at 50. And finally into sight came this lone figure, his legs twirling.

"Who are you?" the stars demanded angrily.

"I'm Jules Banino, an amateur. I'm just riding home at my own pace."

It wasn't the way the best way to put it. The greatest riders in the world had just spent an hour chasing him.

"We don't believe you!" someone shouted. And then a normally mild-mannered and sullen Italian called Ottavio Bottecchia, who had led the Tour from the start and was about to lead it to the end, gave Banino a thump. What was good for Bottecchia, though he barely spoke French and probably hadn't understood Banino anyway, was good for the rest. They joined in and one, the Frenchman Jean Alavoine, kicked Banino into a ditch.

That was misfortune enough. But along the road happened to be a bunch of spectators, all Alavoine supporters. They assumed Banino was the aggressor and their hero the victim. They rounded on Banino as he lay on the ground and gave him a good kicking.

Not many officials traveled with the race and Banino had no team to look out for him. Cycling, like boxing, was for men who'd have been fighting in bars had they not been scrapping on the road. What difference one fight more or less? Banino had already been thrown out of the Tour after hardships imposed by dust-dragging cars. To be attacked when innocent, then kicked and hit by sticks, finally beaten up all over again by supporters whose business it had never been in the first place, was dispiriting. He lay in the ditch for several hours and then recovered enough to ride home. He never rode the Tour de France again.

Altogether more fortunate was the Baron Henri Pépin de Gontaud. And this is the other Dargassies story. In the spring of 1907, the story says, the baron called the valets of his château outside Toulouse and told them they would ride the Tour de France, pacing him at whatever speed he thought gentlemanly and, if necessary, mend his tires and clean his clothes. In return, they would stay at the best hotels and dine at the finest restaurants. He would pay them the 4,000 francs the winner would receive and they would all go home when they'd had enough.

Henri took the train to Paris with his valets and joined the peloton of 112 at the Porte Bineau on July 8. The race started at 5:30am. Pépin, rider 59, had no wish to mix it with ruffians. He preferred to lift his boater to ladies and blow kisses in the air. He finished his conversation with a lady, turned to his valets, and said: "Let us depart. But remember—we have all the time in the world." The bunch had already vanished on its eight-hour ride to Roubaix.

The three never separated. They took 12 hours, 20 minutes longer than Émile Georget from Roubaix to Metz and the judges were furious. The race was decided not on time but points, so they had to wait for everyone. One day the trio came across a man in a ditch. "My name is Jean-Marie Teychenne," the wretch said. "Like you, I am a *coursier*. But I have suffered the most terrible *fringale* [hunger knock]. Leave me, I'm done for."

Pépin recognized the nasal singsong of a fellow Toulousain, a man who said *veng* for *vin* and Toulous-*uh* for Toulouse. "Nonsense," he shouted, and he waited as the valets pulled him up. "You will join us. We live well. We may not win, but we shall see France." And did they finish? Well, no. Somewhere between Lyon and Grenoble on stage five, Pépin decided he'd had a lovely time, paid the money he'd promised and set off for the train to Toulouse. And so ended one of the most colorful incidents of Tour history. And one of its most enduring.

The truth, sadly, isn't as good. The root of the tale is a village called Gontaud-de-Nogaret. It's closer to Bordeaux than Toulouse. And there, Henri Pépin had a heavy wooden trunk painted "Pépin Gontaud Lot et Garonne" in gold script. There is no château at Gontaud-de-Nogaret. Or, if there is, it never belonged to Pépin. He was, though, a man of independent means. The bit about valets and hotels and restaurants and kissing ladies is true. Except that the valets were experienced riders, Dargassies and Henri Gauban. They were the Tour's first *domestiques*, employed in the service of others. Reporters were impressed, saw the inscription on the trunk and took it for a highfalutin' name—Pépin-de-Gontaud—and not an address. It took only further license to make him an aristocrat, a baron.

Pépin, far from a dilettante, had ridden seven stages of the Tour in 1905. He was an established racer with his pictures in magazines. A picture on the cover of *Le Cycle* in October, 1894, shows a lean young man with intense eyes, a weak chin and a twizzled mustache. Studio pictures show him in Oscar Wilde-like pose of gentlemen-displaying-their-calves. And he was rich enough not to sully his hands. Desgrange wrote to him on August 31, 1907: "Dear Mr Pépin, it is with the greatest pleasure that, according to the desire you expressed in your last letter, instead of sending you cash for the allowances owed to you, *L'Auto* will provide you with a medal to the same value." The normally formal Desgrange signed himself *votre bien dévoué*, almost "your fan."

Pépin had ridden the 1905 Tour and so had Dargassies and Gauban. It was probably there they forged their alliance. The confusion with valets probably came from the condescending attitude a rich man would have shown a mere artisan. Pépin rode the Tour for a third time in 1914 and died of athleticism that same year. And what's athleticism? People died of all sorts of things in those days. Whatever it was, it took one of the Tour's great characters.

5

Les Forcats De La Route

*Liberté, égalité, fraternité…*The motto of the French republic since the end of the nineteenth century. It had been used informally since the Revolution back in 1789 but you have only to see the way Desgrange and others ran races to see it was a fine idea but not one to share with the common man.

Desgrange forced riders to tackle huge distances and fined them if they cared to complain. Negotiation wasn't his style. In that he wasn't unusual. In 1892, for instance, ten years before the Tour but when Desgrange was already writing about cycling, Michelin organized a 400-kilometre race from Paris to Clermont-Ferrand, where it made tires. Michelin had just invented a bike tire that could be taken off the rim with relative ease to replace or mend the inner tube. It still took five minutes to detach the outer cover but for other makes it took half an hour and the intervention of a mechanic.

Michelin had these removable tires and its English rival, Dunlop, didn't. The problem was that Michelin's superiority would pass unnoticed if nobody flatted. What more obvious, then, than scatter 25 kilograms of seven-pointed nails on the road? But even then a Michelin rider didn't win. The first over the line was Auguste Stéphane, first winner of the professional Bordeaux–Paris. But he was riding Dunlops and that wasn't good enough. So the Michelin brothers' judges threw him out for changing his bikes several times. They gave the victory instead to a Michelin rider, the Parisian Henri Farman. That's the brother of Maurice Farman, by the way, the man who invented tactics in cycling.

If organizers could throw nails on the road, what couldn't they do? In 1925 Desgrange tried to force every rider in Paris–Tours to eat precisely the same quantity and quality of food. By then riders had a trade union and he was beaten back. The moment that triggered the union was an episode in 1924 when the leading French rider, Henri Pélissier, rode out of the race because an official wouldn't let him take off a jersey when the day grew hotter.

Pélissier was notoriously unpleasant although in the end he shaped the Tour and changed the way riders trained. His story is that in the middle of August, 1911, as a twenty-year-old whom friends called *Ficelle*, he took a day off from his parents' cattle farm—where his father had forbidden him to live in the family house—to go into Paris. *Ficelle* means string. It's also the thinnest of bread sticks, so you can guess how spindly the young farm hand looked.

On August 15, Pélissier was walking close to the Buffalo vélodrome, full of his own thoughts, when he turned at the sound of his name. He saw a sun-darkened man with a floppy mustache. His adopted name was Lucien Petit-Breton.

Petit-Breton's real name was Mazan. His father, a disgraced politician who fled France for Argentina and returned only cautiously, considered enough dark clouds had been dragged through the family's sky. He forbade his son to ride bike races.

"To him, to ride a bicycle was to bring dishonor on the family name," Lucien said. "So the first time I raced, without my parents' knowing of course, I was asked my name and of course I hesitated. I said 'Breton… I'm a Breton' [meaning he came from Brittany]. But it turned out there was already someone else in the race called Breton, so because I was younger they entered me as Petit-Breton." And so his career began, as Lucien Petit-Breton, the little Breton. By the time it ended he had won the Tour de France twice, in 1907 and 1908. He may have gone on to more but like Faber, Lapize (shot down as a fighter pilot) and so many stars of his generation, he died during the first world war.

"Want to come to Italy with me?" Petit-Breton asked. Pélissier looked as startled as you'd imagine. To Pélissier, Petit-Breton was a hero. It was like being hailed by Greg LeMond or Eddy Merckx.

"To Italy? To do what?" In 1911, when so few people left their village that dialects a few hours apart were incomprehensible, it was impossibly romantic.

"To race, of course. It's three o'clock. The train for Milan goes at nine. Make your mind up."

They took the train. A few days later they were riding the Tour of Romany–Tuscany. As it happened, Henri crashed and didn't finish.

But the experience did him no harm because he won Turin–Florence–Rome and then the Tour of Lombardy. He won Lombardy the following year as well, crashing at the entrance to the horse track in Milan with Costante Girardengo, the star of the day. A heap of riders came down with them with just two 400-metre laps of the track to ride. Girardengo's fans were furious and set about Pélissier with their fists, so that he had scramble three metres up the judges' watchtower and wait for 80 policemen to quell the mob below him.

Pélissier came second in his first Tour de France in 1914, less than two minutes behind Philippe Thys of Belgium. He took three stages: the tenth, twelfth and fifteenth. He argued repeatedly with Desgrange, which wasn't difficult for either of them. Desgrange penalized him two minutes for leaving a flat tire by the roadside in 1920 and Pélissier left the race in protest. He then made a point of winning everywhere else for the rest of the season. Did it work? No it didn't. Desgrange scoffed: "Pélissier can win any race except the Tour."

He, his brother Francis and a little-known Parisian, Maurice Ville, abandoned the 1924 Tour at Coutances, on the northwest coast, after an official wouldn't let him take off a jersey. They sulked in the station café—no longer there because the Allied invasion flattened the town—and spilled the beans to a celebrated journalist called Albert Londres.

"Had a bang?"

"No," says Henri. "It's just that we're not dogs."

"What's happened?"

"A question of jerseys. This morning at Cherbourg, the commissaire [André Trialoux, a busybody and bully] approached me and, without saying anything, he lifted my jersey. He was checking that I didn't have the wrong number of jerseys. What would you do if I lifted your jacket to see if you had a white shirt? I didn't like his manners, that's all."

"What would have happened if you'd had two jerseys?

"I could have had fifteen, but I don't have the right to start with two and finish with only one."

"Why?"

"It's the rule. It's not enough that we should race like brutes, we also have to freeze or stifle."

Pélissier stormed off to see Desgrange. They had a good row and Pélissier rode off, taking his brother and, for some reason, Maurice Ville.

"You have no idea what the Tour de France is," Pélissier told Londres. "We suffer on the road. But do you want to see how we keep going? Wait…" He took a phial from his bag. "That, that's cocaine for our eyes and chloroform for our gums… And pills? You want to see the pills?"

They got out three boxes apiece.

"In short," said Francis, "we run on dynamite."

Remembering the standardized food, he said Desgrange would one day insist riders carry stones to make them heavier. Londres had the best color piece he'd written. *Le Petit Parisien* on June 30, 1924, headlined it *Les Forçats de la Route*, a reference to chain gangs forced to break rocks. Francis claimed they exaggerated to take advantage of his gullibility. But it couldn't be bettered as mischief.

Pélissier was popular with fans but riders were more guarded. The more aggrieved joined him, happy to fight life's pinpricks. The level-headed kept their distance, not sure they wanted to be represented by a rider who "treated every organizer and every factory [sponsor] as an enemy," as Desgrange phrased it. The union fought off identical food and then collapsed.

Where Pélissier succeeded, other than winning the Tour at 34 in 1923, was in insisting cycling should be speed rather than endurance. He was the first obsessive, sandpapering his wooden rims—for years Desgrange banned metal rims for fear they would overheat and shed tires on descents—to save 50 grams. "On a moving part that's worth two kilos on the frame," he told a journalist who surprised him.

He trained early in the day with what we'd now recognise as interval training. In the afternoon he went out with the boys, telling them: "It's important not to wear yourself out" but never letting on that he'd been out at dawn for 40 kilometres' speed training. It gave him speed and denied it to others, although he was rarely tactful. "They are cart horses and I am a thoroughbred," he said one summer. Next day he stopped with a flat tire and the entire race attacked, leaving him and Francis 30 minutes down.

He argued constantly with Desgrange, about anything but often the length of stages. "What is the point of making them so long that we can't race?" he asked. And he had a point because they could be 360 kilometres. Riders drank wine and sniffed ether from handkerchiefs beneath their chins, simply to dull the pain. They began drinking with their heavy breakfasts, which made them sluggish. The Pélissiers rarely drank and never ate a lot in the morning—which was when they attacked. Desgrange did eventually see that the further riders rode, the less they raced. They stayed together in a truce, riding as slowly as they could get away with, to get to the finish. Only in the last hour did they get going.

Pélissier was ahead of his time but his life was never happy. Maybe it was conceit at so much talent, of being the sort of man who gets hailed in the street by Tour de France winners, a man whom stars take to Italy on a whim. Léonie, his wife, despaired of him and shot herself in 1933. Three years later Henri took a lover, Camille Tharault, who was twenty years younger. He loved her and called her Miette but their life was row after row. On May 1, 1935, in the kitchen of their villa at Dampierre, outside Paris, Pélissier lunged with a knife, cutting her face. She ran in tears to their bedroom, pulled out the revolver with which Léonie had shot herself, ran back to the kitchen and found Pélissier waiting with the knife.

She pulled the trigger five times. A bullet hit him in the carotid artery and blood spurted across the room. His body was placed in the room where Léonie had killed herself. Next day, *Paris-Soir* screamed

THE TRAGIC END
OF HENRI PÉLISSIER
surprises no-one at Dampierre
'If I'd had the money I would
have left him long ago' the
murderess said yesterday

Camille's trial opened a year later. She pleaded self-defence and got a year's suspended jail sentence. It was as close as the court could come to acquitting her.

Pélissier is just a name in history these days. But he's not forgotten. At the entrance to the Piste Municipale in Paris, one of the oldest tracks in Europe, is a bas-relief of him and his brothers, Charles and Francis. It was commissioned and paid for by spectators grateful for the pride they brought France.

6

The Swoop Of The Kingfisher

Desgrange was nothing if not complicated. He stood for simple ideas, purity and clarity of behavior. And yet his race reports had journalistically corrupt phrases such as "the riders fought their battle with the mountains while the judges followed in cars which, thanks to Benz carburetors, could master the ascent while lesser cars struggled."

This wasn't by chance. Desgrange and his journalists sat on the upper floor of 10 Faubourg-Montmartre. Goddet sat downstairs with the bookkeepers and the advertising people. Messengers carried notes between the two. *L'Auto* once wrote of a driver "in a Renault using Michelin tires with the agreement of the first floor." The story had gone downstairs to be approved by the advertising department. The sales staff, to keep in with Renault and Michelin, had agreed. The reporter, to avoid trouble, penciled "with the agreement of the first floor" in the margin and the typesetter had printed it.

Desgrange, you'll remember, was a buddy of John Varmm Hammond of La Française. Because of that he either instructed Lefèvre to show preference to Hammond's star, Maurice Garin, or he let Lefèvre think he'd be in trouble if he didn't. La Française was one of a handful of factories which employed all the stars among them. Until the 1950s teams were backed in their entirety from within the industry and outside sponsors were neither allowed nor sought. The biggest were Peugeot in blue and yellow, La Française in scarlet, and Alcyon in kingfisher blue. If Desgrange leaned towards one then he must have leaned away from the others. And the team that annoyed him most was Alcyon.

Alcyon began making bikes in 1902 in a factory at Neuilly-sur-Seine, the area of Paris northwest from the Arc de Triomphe. Its founder was Edmond Gentil, who had walked out from Peugeot after a row.

Peugeot sold bikes by sponsoring professionals and Gentil opened fire in return. His riders won fourteen Tours, twelve Paris–Roubaix, thirteen Bordeaux–Paris and dozens of championships.

Gentil wasn't gentle. He employed managers with brio. The first was Alphonse Baugé, better known as a Peugeot manager, and the next Ludo Feuillet, a man in a white top and circular gold-rimmed glasses whose background as a medical student accustomed to him to blood. His team became known as *La Taule*, the prison.

Feuillet made Alcyon the world's best, but riders trembled at his style. He once drove Marcel Bidot into a hedge so a more favored team member could win. The French journalist Gérard Ejnès said Alcyon "crushed the 1909 Tour, taking thirteen of its fourteen stages, five in a row (going from 259 to 398 kilometres), from the second to the sixth, between Roubaix and Nice, providing a winner [François Faber] who, the press of the time reported, never once weakened throughout 4,488 kilometres. Nobody would go as far as saying he achieved such an exploit on just water, but in those days everything was permitted."

Alcyon didn't manage that without teamwork. Desgrange accepted teams but forbade teamwork. His was to be a race of individuals. The riders had long learned about pacing each other: the reason they never seem to be doing it in pictures is that they didn't care to be caught. Desgrange did his best to catch truants. And in 1911 he did.

The debonair Maurice Brocco, known as Coco, rode for Alcyon. He inadvertently created the word *domestique* for a rider employed to help others. Brocco lost so much time on the stage to Chamonix that he could no longer win. He told his teammate, François Faber—the man who won two years earlier—that he'd help him get through a bad day. And he paced him.

Desgrange spotted him and wanted to throw him out. He'd suspected him for a while. He couldn't prove it though and, for all his power, he worried Brocco would complain to the *Union Vélocipèdique Française*. He vented his opinions in *L'Auto*, sneering that Brocco "is unworthy. He is no more than a *domestique*," a household servant.

Brocco wasn't amused. Next day he confronted Desgrange and warned: "Today, *monsieur*, we are going to settle accounts." He set off with the eventual winner, Gustave Garrigou, as they started on the Tourmalet. Desgrange watched from his car. "So, do you forbid me to ride with him?" Brocco shouted. They went over the Tourmalet and then began the Aubisque. He dropped Garrigou and caught the day's leader, Émile Georget. Desgrange was still there. Brocco sneered again. "So, then, am I allowed to stay with him?" And to prove he didn't need to ride with anyone whether Desgrange gave permission or not, he cleared off and won by 34 minutes.

Desgrange had witnessed a great ride. But he made a connection which Brocco overlooked. If Brocco could ride so well one day, he could only have ridden poorly the day before by coming to a deal with Faber. Therefore he must be guilty. "He deserves his punishment," wrote the organizer, commissaire and chief executioner. "Immediate disqualification."

Desgrange had been frustrated since the start—first by riders who refused to race flat out every second, then by the way they combined as individuals or as teams. If he judged the race on elapsed time, as it is now, a single mishap could cost a rider the Tour. Given that officials once penalized Eugène Christophe because a boy helped pump the

Drama on the road: outside Sainte-Marie-de-Campan at the foot of the Tourmalet, Eugène Christophe was forced to weld his own bicycle together or be forced from the race.

forge on which he was forced to weld his broken forks, that was no small consideration. On the other hand, if he judged the race on points, the order in which riders finished rather than the time they took, riders ambled until the last hour. If someone broke away, they weren't inclined to chase because it made no difference how much lead he got.

The day after the Tour finished in 1926, he complained about riders and their laziness, blamed team managers for weakness, accused factories of breaking contracts, journalists of criticizing his race. Above all, he railed at riders: "What we call a *métier*, in other words the need to work that weighs heavily on humanity, has turned into a search to do everything with the least effort. 'What's the point', the riders say, 'of wearing ourselves out when it's not absolutely necessary? The Tour lasts a month. It's not going to last a day less just because we ride like crazy on all the stages. So let's wait until we have no choice; let's wait for the Alps and the Pyrenees.' So, you'll notice, the Tour de France has become the Tour de France only when it's in the mountains."

If riders intended to fall asleep on seventeen stages, he had the solution. All but the six days through the mountains—where riders deigned to race—and three significant days on the flat would be team time-trials. Why not run all the stages against the clock? Because that way there would be no individual winner.

The hybrid impressed nobody. A financial crisis was crossing Europe and several bike companies took the chance to stay away. That kept out Automoto and Lucien Buysse, third in 1924, second in 1925 and winner in 1926. The result was predictable: the stronger teams dominated, all the more because alone on the road they couldn't attack and outwit each other. They were free to ride flat out, as Desgrange wanted, but that just increased the distance between them and weaker teams. Individuals press-ganged into small teams by circumstance were outclassed. Nicolas Frantz, for Alcyon, won by 1 hour, 48 minutes. The first non-Alcyon rider was 4 hours, 48 minutes behind.

Anyone else would have admitted his error. Not Desgrange. If a bad idea didn't work then a worse one might. If teams lost men exhausted by unequal competition, they could bring in replacements, including riders who'd already dropped out. Arsène Alancourt and Francis Boullet, for instance, started the stage to Luchon by bike and then climbed into a passing truck. The truck slid off the road and they finished the stage in a taxi. Three days later they rejoined the Tour, riding for the same team.

No team was stronger than its weakest rider, which put extra strain on the stars and stopped their succeeding. The best rider in a weak team could be useful to any rival team that passed him on the road, as he would be likely to jump in with them and leave his own team. That further weakened the poor team and added an extra pair of legs to the stronger. And into that parody of a race came a small group of Australians and New Zealanders anxious at what they'd been asked to do. There had been Australians in the Tour before: Don Kirkham and Iddo Munro came seventeenth and twentieth in 1914 and of them there'll be more later. But this was a team with a weight on its shoulders because readers of the *Melbourne Herald* and *Sporting Globe* in Australia and the *Sun* in New Zealand had raised £1,200 to send them.

The idea was that Hubert Opperman, Percy Osborne, Frankie Thomas, Ernie Bainbridge and the New Zealander Harry Watson would ride with six Frenchmen to be found by Charles Proctor, the manager of the small French bike company, Ravat, which was to sponsor them. The Europeans never materialized, never having heard of the plan, so the southerners rode alone against teams twice as large and a thousand times more experienced. They were the first English-speaking team in the Tour.

The London *Daily Telegraph* called Opperman "a rather nondescript figure, barely of middle height and weight, with a homely face, but he was marked by an unquenchable spirit, a genuine modesty, and a cheerful simplicity of manner." He was a long-distance specialist, said Pierre Chany, "but his companions were notoriously less gifted."

The five reached Paris ambitious but obvious hicks. Jonathan Kennett wrote in his biography of Watson: "The Australasians trained with the French Olympic team—fifteen amateurs who were treated better than the best Antipodean professionals. The French thoroughbreds laughed at the balloon tires used by the back-country lads. With the French scorn ringing in their ears, Watson and his teammates quickly modeled themselves on their rivals and soon sported narrow tubular tires and new handlebars and clothes—including matching plus-fours and berets."

It was a hideous mismatch.

The Franco-American reporter René De Latour wrote: "Even if I live to be 150 years old, I shall never forget the sight of the poor lonely Opperman being caught day after day by the various teams of ten super-athletes, swapping their pace beautifully. The four Australians [*sic*] would start together. Bainbridge would do his best to hang on, but even though he may have been a good rider in the past, the passing years had taken most of his speed, and he would generally go off the back after 50 miles or so…That left three Aussies against the trade teams' ten. Then, inevitably, if it was not Osborne it was Watson who would have to quit at the 100 miles mark. And almost daily, Oppy would be left alone for the last 50 miles."

The team that usually swept him up was Alcyon. Ludo Feuillet adopted him and gave him tires and other help. Opperman finished the Tour eighteenth, eight and a half hours behind Frantz, the winner for the second time. Read Australian accounts and Feuillet sounds a kindly uncle taking in a stray. Hardly. Feuillet knew just what he was doing. Opperman had talent. Opperman joined Alcyon and won the Bol d'Or 24-hour.

Alcyon won the Tour and Desgrange lost hope. Alcyon had the best riders. It built a lead on the flat that could never be overturned in the mountains. Well, if a team race didn't work, the Tour would return to a race for individuals.

Ludo Feuillet snickered.

7

My Race Has Been Won
By A Corpse

Desgrange's contempt for riders showed. Either they went faster than
30 kilometres per hour, he threatened, or he'd go back to team time-
trials next day. They had been warned. But he should have learned his
lesson. Right from the start, Alcyon employed not only team tactics
but engaged *isolés*—the Tour had two classes of riders supposed to be
riding separate races—with whom it had a link. More than that, the
team paid cash to any rival prepared to help.

Leading Alcyon and leading the Tour was Maurice Dewaele, a
Dutch-speaking Belgian from Lovendegem who had come second
in 1927 and third in 1928. He had, however, fallen ill. Marcel Bidot
was one of Alcyon's riders. He recounted: "There were eight stages left,
taking us over the Galibier, Aravis, the Jura, across the north, from
Metz to Malo-les-Bains, which was a succession of out-of-the-usual
difficulties. Fortunately, the Alcyon team was solid. Dewaele could
count on André Leducq, Nicolas Frantz, Gaston Rebry and me. We
would cut off our arms to help him. However, he was sicker than we
thought. He had a sleepless night in Grenoble, and an hour before the
start, he passed out.

"We pushed him on his bike to send him off to his misery. The opposition, of course, knew all about it. Antonin Magne, of the Alleluia
team, reckoned on attacking right from the start. The race set off along
a wide avenue and so, with his brother Pierre, he made the most of the
darkness to take off along side roads. What he didn't realize was that
we knew, because Jules Moineau had told us. We put our sentries in
place under the banner and blocked the road. It took three hours to
ride 50 kilometres, so you can guess the average speed."

The procession helped Dewaele recover and he began to ride well on the Galibier. He rode well because his teammates pushed him, something Bidot didn't think to add. They pushed him on climb after climb. Desgrange was furious. Whenever he turned up, the pushing stopped. When he told his driver to take his Hotchkiss elsewhere—Desgrange never learned to drive—the pushing began again. And, given Alcyon's open wallet policy, others joined in or didn't object.

"My race has been won by a corpse," Desgrange wailed. "How could a *maillot jaune* so easy to pluck have kept his first place? Why was the opposition so ineffective? What can we make of their tactics and the real worth of the winner?"

Alcyon, of course, feigned hurt innocence. But they had achieved more than make a sick man win: they had contrived themselves—and other sponsors—out of the Tour. Desgrange was tired of his race, or at any rate the way he believed it was abused. He couldn't fight the sponsors, who undermined all his intentions, and he could no longer enthuse the public. Two years of team time-trials had made them yawn. And although there were plenty of good French riders, Belgians were a surer bet and it was Belgians the factories picked as leader. And they had plenty to choose from: Belgium had no bike factories and so its riders rode for French employers. From 1912 to 1929, foreigners won thirteen of the fourteen Tours.

The Tour had a life but its purpose remained to sell *L'Auto* and pay its employees. Just one Frenchman—Henri Pélissier—had won in fourteen years and the French, like all people, bought newspapers most when one of their own did well. Sales of *L'Auto* stuck at 50,000. And then they started going down.

If French riders could be brought together, their strength could be greater than their parts. A national team had potential winners in André Leducq, Antonin Magne and Marcel Bidot, and a stage winner in the dashing, in both senses, Charles Pélissier. Charles, brother of Henri and Francis, was the only Pélissier whom Desgrange could tolerate. Everybody liked Charles. Especially women. They saw something of Beau Brummel, the nineteenth-century dandy. And that was how the papers referred to him.

Desgrange had created a sport—bicycle stage racing—and perfected it. But the harder he tried to make it honest, the more a dictator he had to be. And the more dictatorial he became, the more riders and employers outwitted him. Instead of getting better, the Tour was becoming a farce. Jacques Goddet remembered: "Everything had been tried, in obvious chaos, with every form of encouragement and punishment. The experiments were all carried out in a spirit of permanent revolt against the bike makers. They were responsible for all the Tour's ills. They came from their eagerness to win the Tour, on which their sales depended, by any means. They came from the disparity of their means. So, obviously, they had to be booted out, this scabby riffraff, and above all the monumental Edmond Gentil had to lose his head for wanting to annex bike-racing for himself! I had the privilege of witnessing the anguished somersaults of a man of character who preferred to throw himself into a veritable revolution, with all the risks and above all with all the expenses it would bring, than stay in the grip of the factories."

Victor Goddet had relaunched *L'Auto* several times and in the process become the majority shareholder, making Desgrange his employee. Goddet died in 1926 and, against the law but seemingly with no objection from his sons, left fewer shares to Jacques than to his elder son, Maurice. In the fall of 1929 Desgrange discussed his revolution with Jacques, who approved, then took them to Maurice. And Maurice, more interested in partying, probably said yes with no more than a glance.

From Wednesday, July 2, 1930, the Tour would be for France, Belgium, Italy, Spain and Germany in groups of eight. "Why [just] five national teams?" Desgrange asked. "Because only five countries are in a position to provide a team: Belgium, Italy, Spain, Germany and France. Luxembourg has only one man. Switzerland has only three. Austria just one. The other countries have none at all. Why teams of eight? I'm going to whisper something in your ear, confidentially. If you've got several hundred thousand francs that aren't doing anything, we can maybe increase the teams to twelve."

The size and publicity of the Tour obliged factories to release their riders. They said they didn't like it but hindsight shows they didn't mind: getting their best men into the Tour without having to pay for them in a worldwide recession saved a lot of money. To make up spaces liberated by Tour riders, they took on replacements given only a bike, a jersey and any bonuses they might gain, a system called riding *à la musette*. It put a lot of extra riders on the road, all wearing advertising at better than cut-price rates, and it undermined professional cycling for decades.

What troubled the factories more was Desgrange's insistence that riders not use their own bikes. Instead, the eight national teams and a further nine representing French regions would present their saddles and handlebars 48 hours before the start and mechanics would fit them to anonymous frames painted yellow to match *L'Auto* and labeled only with the paper's name. In keeping with the era and the Tour's rules, the bikes were steel throughout and had no derailleur and, despite their introduction, no alloy rims. Desgrange thought derailleurs corrupted competition and that prolonged braking on mountain descents would melt the glue that held the tires. There was no double chainring, either, for that hadn't been invented. Instead, riders chose a 46 or 48-tooth ring and fitted a three-speed freewheel with 16, 17 and 18 teeth for the flat and 22, 23, 25 for the climbs. Changing gears still required a rider to stop, jump off and fiddle with his back wheel just as he did in the days of single gears that had no freewheel.

Desgrange, so adamant the Tour should be pure of team tactics, had created a race which could be anything but. But he had dynamited Gentil and anything was worth that. Alcyon itself lasted until 1954, when it was bought by Peugeot, and the team ended two years later. Gentil died at the start of the 1960s.

Desgrange had to discuss the costs with the Goddet brothers. Some would come from an expected rise in *L'Auto*'s sales. More would come from bike factories unable to resist advertising their riders' performances, even on yellow bikes. Those bikes, incidentally, were made by Alcyon; Feuillet leaked that to the press. And then there was the enterprising Paul Thévenin, publicity man of the Menier chocolates company. It started in 1856 and reached its peak in the 1930s. After the war, it suffered from chocolate imported from the USA as a condition of Marshall Aid, changed hands several times and is now part of the Swiss giant, Nestlé.

Thévenin wasn't the first to spot that driving along with a bike race exposed spectators to his advertising. The pioneer was probably the Parisian department store, Galéries Lafayette, which joined in with Bordeaux–Paris in 1922. But Menier had something to throw to the crowds—his chocolate. His only problem was that nobody knew he was there if he preceded the race; officials wouldn't let him drive *with* the race and most spectators would have gone home if he followed it.

Desgrange told Thévenin that, for a fee, he could drive just ahead of the riders. The crowd in an era without television would be at its densest. He did the same deal with La Vache Qui Rit, Graf, Biscottes Delft, Esders and Noveltex. Menier was delighted and so was the crowd: his staff threw out tons of chocolate and half a million policeman's hats printed with the firm's name. They made hot chocolate for fans, riders and officials in the mountains. Menier gave 5,000 francs to the first rider to the top of cols. He had the biggest publicity budget of any company in France, according to Pierre Chany, and he made the most of it. It was such a success that Desgrange had little trouble recruiting other companies when he took twenty of their representatives to lunch. Perrier, Pernod, Martini and Banania stayed for decades.

Every vehicle in the caravan tried to be cleverer, louder and of still less taste than the others. They yelled of "the mint alcohol of Ricqlès, which stimulates, refreshes and comforts" and "Byrrh—the drink that sportsmen prefer." Lucky Strike went further. Not only did it shout about cigarettes "which don't hurt your throat or make you cough" but it pictured André Leducq smoking beside the caption "I like Lucky Strike." Before long the drinks companies expanded into the evening as well, holding street parties with popular singers such as Tino Rossi and Charles Trenet.

Desgrange felt pleased. He had routed the bike factories. He had saved the Tour. And he had arranged to have his costs paid by companies outside the sport and by the cities his race visited. What he hadn't foreseen was that those companies would, within a couple of decades and against the Tour's wishes, take over the sport in a way the bike factories couldn't have imagined. But by then Desgrange was dead and the problems fell to others.

Part Three: Echappée Matinale

Almost every stage of the modern Tour starts with an attack in the first kilometres. The race still has a long way to go and the hopefuls are usually allowed their lead until well into the afternoon, when they are swallowed up. They are known as the "echappée matinale", or the "morning break."

1
An Era Dawns

The American cycling boom was weakening. Major Taylor died forgotten and broke and was buried in a pauper's grave. The professional
track circus was faltering. Tracks had car license plates over gouges for
lack of money to fix them properly. The end came with the Wall Street
crash in October, 1929, and vélodromes were abandoned or pulled
down. Just before the crash, America was due to hold the world cycling championships.

The *Union Cycliste Internationale*, across the Atlantic, knew little
but good of American cycling. It had seen American stars mop up
Europeans and fill seats with their glamour. It knew the six-day circuit
was richer than any race on earth and that that was where the best Europeans were drawn. What it possibly didn't know was that by the end
of the 1920s there was little other racing in America worth celebrating.

The administrative body, USA Cycling, has one of its roots in the
Amateur Bicycle League of America, renamed the United States Cycling Federation in 1975. The Amateur League began in 1920 to revive the moribund state of cycling away from professional tracks. The
showman of the pro world was John Chapman, in Peter Nye's words
"a stiff-looking man in a starched white shirt and collar, his tie always
in place, wearing a business suit, button shoes, and rimless eyeglasses."
He was, says Nye, "notoriously tightfisted with money." Chapman's
novelty, says his entry for the US Bicycling Hall of Fame, was that "he
set the world five-mile tandem record in 1901 which stood for 50 years."

Chapman ran the National Cycling Association, which allowed
racing on Sunday when the League of American Wheelmen didn't.
Chapman and the NCA were interested only in professional track racing and didn't welcome the arrival of the ABLA. Lawsuits followed
and pressure was applied to stop racing spreading to the road, but in

time both sides settled down and Chapman remained, as Nye put it, "a quiet, soft speaking, czar of the sport in America."

The NCA was America's representative to the UCI. And in 1927, the UCI told Frank Kramer, the chairman of the NCA's controlling committee, that America was to run the 1929 world championships. Kramer had pointed to the last championships held in the USA, in 1912, and promised that the same man—Chapman—would be in charge.

The UCI remembered not only Chapman but that Kramer had won the sprint. And, incidentally, the American sprint championship for sixteen years. He had only just stopped racing when he put America's case to the UCI.

The races in 1912 were only on the track—six laps to the mile in South Orange Avenue in Newark—and only for women. By 1929, the UCI had road as well as track championships—the first professional road race was 1927—and Chapman would be expected to promote both. He wasn't inclined to. He'd run the track races, he said, but not the road. When the UCI wanted a cut of the gate, Chapman lost interest in the championships and the UCI lost interest in America. Look at the records and you'll see no mention of Newark: the championships passed to Zürich in Switzerland. Everyone who took part was in at least his 70s by the time the UCI gave the races to America again.

The footnote is that Newark vélodrome, where the dream began, lasted only a year longer. The lease expired in 1930 and nobody sought to renew it. Fans campaigned for a replacement and the mayor joined them. But wreckers moved in and demolished it. The rival track at Coney Island burned down the same year.

As for Britain, there was true symbolism when Jacques Goddet rode into Oxford on a racing bike and his friends on roadsters with rod brakes. France and the European continent never lost interest in cycling. The English-speaking nations did. The British went further and shot themselves in the foot. Their National Cyclists' Union championships, until the International Cycling Association, were de facto championships of the world. But just as Marshal Taylor was at his peak, the NCU cast its members into cycling darkness for half a century. Like many an unwise decision, it concerned a woman.

On July 21, 1894, she was conducting her horse and carriage 60 miles north of London when she got tangled up in a 50-mile cycling race. In those days races were conducted with pacers so that for every competitor there was a string of riders. The woman's horse reared and pushed all the passing cyclists into a ditch. Nobody was hurt but there was offense on both sides. The woman said she would protest to the chief constable. The position of all cyclists was uncertain. The NCU worried a law could end all cycling and it banned clubs from organizing road races and its members from taking part. They were to ride on the track instead.

The point the NCU missed was that there weren't enough tracks. A rebel organization therefore promoted secret races at dawn, riders dressed "inconspicuously" from head to toe in black, starting a minute apart. The competitions were called time-trials so as not to breathe the word "race." Before long both bodies got along fine and repelled all further change.

The NCU wasn't against road racing. It just didn't want it unless it was on closed roads such as airfields. Abroad was fine. British riders were invited to the first Bordeaux–Paris in 1891 because of their reputation for endurance racing. The NCU gave permission provided there'd be no professionals. An amateur who rode against a professional became a professional himself. This wasn't the French view. The French meaning of *amateur* was someone who did something because he enjoyed it. Provided he didn't win a living wage, he couldn't survive on cycling and he stayed an amateur.

The British demanded nevertheless that not a coin must fall and the French gave in, delighted to have their pioneering race made international. They thought it would take two days and laid on meals and beds. The British took the first four places in barely more than a day, which meant a lot of untouched meals from the Garonne to the capital. The NCU, you'd think, would be delighted. But it observed that its winner, George Mills, worked for the Humber bicycle company near Nottingham. And he had to prove that Humber hadn't paid so much as a postage stamp towards his entry, without which he would be ruled a professional. And, because there were no professional races and no way back to being an amateur, he would be forced out of cycling.

The blinkers stayed on, not simply on amateurism but on racing on the road generally, until a pirate group called the British League of Racing Cyclists rebelled on the empty roads of the second world war and promoted races regardless. The civil war between the NCU and

BLRC lasted until, exhausted and close to bankrupt, they merged in 1959.

Among those the NCU sent to the 1932 Los Angeles Olympics was a dark-eyed man from Birmingham, in the center of England: Charles Holland. "The dusky Midlander", one paper called him. The Olympics suited him because the road race was run as at home, as a time-trial. He went on *Empress of Britain* in a group pared because of cost to those sure of getting to a semifinal. He came fifteenth on the road and third in the team pursuit. In 1934 Britain sent him to the world championship in Leipzig, where the marshals were Brownshirts, members of Hitler's *Sturmabteilung*. The manager had spent his cycling life at Herne Hill vélodrome in south London and knew little of road racing. Despite that and three broken spokes, Holland came fourth.

He held on as an amateur until the Berlin Olympics in 1936. That brought him no medals and he turned professional to ride a six-day in Wembley, north London, promoted by a Canadian entrepreneur and former track star, Willy Spencer. And then he entered the Tour de France in 1937, Goddet's first complete Tour as organizer. In a video interview, he said: "My interest came from the number of riders I'd met who'd ridden it, and I felt that if they could do it then so could I. I had the best massed-start experience of any rider in the country because I'd won races such as the one in the Isle of Man, which was pretty tough because of its mountainous nature. They seemed very pleased to get my entry, the Tour de France. They thought I wouldn't stand it, that only a real professional could do it. I sent off my entry and I got a very good reply and they offered me this and that so I agreed."

The Isle of Man is an island off northwest England. While a British protectorate, it is a distinct nation. Neither the population nor the police having fears about cyclists, the Manx began a week of cycling races known popularly as the Bicycle TT, after the motorcycle races. If Goddet had read what happened, he might not have been so keen. Only world championship riders had ridden a road circuit. The rest knew no more than airfields and some not that. Now they were on streets that twisted and turned through suburbs, then looped round the island along roads that changed direction and width and passed over humped bridges. The course went over a mountain, down a long descent and, at the bottom of it just before the finish, round a tight looping turn round a picturesque bridge.

Eight crashed in a few hundred yards. A load more came down shortly afterwards when two riders changed direction suddenly. A rider hit a motorcycle sidecar and there was another crash at Glen Helen. Two more fell near Kirk Michael and another ten when someone's chain broke. There were crashes at The Bungalow, Keppel Gate and Creg-ny-Baa—all landmarks on the TT course. A Londoner, Reg Green, hit a stone wall and broke his nose. Another jammed his chain going round the Governors Bridge hairpin and ran the last mile. By the end, 31 had fallen off in 38 miles, from a field of 81. Two had broken collarbones and six needed other hospital treatment. Britain was decidedly not a road-racing nation.

2
Foreigners Abroad

Knowing none of this, Goddet took Holland's entry and lumped him in with a Londoner, Bill Burl, and Canadian Pierre Gachon, both as unknown as Holland. They were to ride for the British Empire, Holland and Burl the first Britons in the Tour and Gachon the first Canadian. Burl went to Belgium to race and train, and crashed in Ostend and broke a collarbone. Gachon started the Tour and was dropped on the first climb and abandoned. Burl fell so far behind on the second day that the organizers threw him out. Holland rode for 2,000 miles until he punctured 30 metres behind the leaders on the col de Port. He started work on a new tire but the heat had warped his pump and made it useless.

He got it to half-pressure but punctured twice more and ran out of tires. Nobody would help. He stood by the roadside in despair. "A crowd of peasants had gathered around me," he said, "but they couldn't help me. A priest brought me a bottle of beer, and although it quenched my thirst it got me no further. After I had given up hope, a tourist came along and gave me a tubular touring tire. I put it on, and in the excitement of the moment the rod of the pump broke. We blew the tire hard with another pump but the tire fitted so loosely on the rim that it came off with the fingers and so was unsafe. Another tire was found that fitted a little better, and again I set off, but I had by then given up hope."

Belgian journalists including Karel van Wijnendaele, the founder of the Tour of Flanders, refused to take him in their car, knowing it would mean disqualification. They offered spare tires instead and pushed him as they drove. In the end he accepted a lift from someone else and became a footnote in the Tour. French spectators were disappointed. One, from Lacelle in the thinly populated Corrèze region, had written: "My dear Holland, I am a French girl who likes very much her bicycle and who is very fond of 'Tour de France'. So, I read '*L'Auto*' and I listen to 'Radio-Luxembourg'. I have been very pleased to learn we would have an English '*équipe*' this year. First, I congratulate you for this: to run the 'Tour de France' because I know it is not very important in England, your people prefers tennis, golf and so on, and however not one other competition permits as well as this, to measure courage. I think you have come with your own will and I say it is very well indeed. Unhappily, your friends have had no luck, and it is very bad for you too, because it must be so hard to stay alone, in a so hard performance. So I admire your 'war' and all my best thoughts on the 'Tour de France' are for you. Don't be sorry if you are not the first, it is impossible when one is alone."

Journalists did him proud: they reported next morning that peasants had pushed him in relays from one village to the next to get him started again. Which goes to show you should never believe everything you read in papers. Not that you'd have read much in Britain. *The Times* never mentioned Holland and Burl. Its only references to the Tour as a whole were two separate paragraphs headed "Discordant cycle race: pepper thrown at Belgian team" and "France wins Tour de France."

Holland recalled: "You need a manager for a race like that, someone who can hand up your rations and your drinks, which you get through a lot of. But to have an organization for one man wasn't in their thinking. They thought that nobody could ride without a manager. So they got all the publicity they could out of me but they wanted me out because what would people think if an individual rider with no support finished their race?" He died in December 1989 and he's buried in the family grave at Aldridge in Staffordshire.

Pierre Gachon, the first North American to ride the Tour, had made his name around Montreal more as a track rider than a roadie. The Canadians were as mystified by the British riders in the Empire trio as they were about Gachon. What made his position more exotic was that he had been born not in Canada but in Paris, France, on March 9, 1909. His father died in world war one. His mother then married a garage owner in the Dutch-speaking half of Belgium. The car business looked better in Montreal and so they emigrated.

Pierre wasn't a cyclist but another Belgian expatriate, Jules Matton, was. Matton got him cycling and Gachon rode the Montreal six-days, coming fourth in April and October 1931, then fifth in 1933 and 1936 paired with his brother, Louis. He won a stage of the Transcanada on the road in 1936 and set long-distance road records. The idea that he should ride the Tour came from the magazine *Bicycles*. Like Holland and Burl, he entered individually. Where they had only the hour and a half of the Channel ferry, Gachon left Quebec on June 12 aboard the *Emperor of Australia* and reached France eight days later.

A training ride on the cobbles of the north shook him, physically and morally. He weighed just 138 pounds and they bounced him everywhere. "There is no *pavé* in Canada," he explained. "It gave me quite a shock. And I need to get used to riding with a derailleur because at home we ride on a fixed wheel."

The riders collected outside *L'Auto* between 5:30 and 7:30am. Gachon was overwhelmed and impressed that his British companions were so calm that they'd visited the World's Exhibition on the banks of the Seine. At 9am the race started by rolling along the Champs Élysées to the Arc de Triomphe and on to Le Vésinet on the outskirts. The finish was on the horse track in Lille, seven hours and 263 kilometres away.

Four riders went ahead on the côte du Pecq, the first hill—and Gachon went out the back. *Miroir des Sports* reported: "Let us bury straight away this poor Gachon, unique victim of the first stage. Straight after the start, since he was already well dropped, we got up beside him to ask what was wrong. But instead of answering in the language of Shakespeare, the Canadian replied in Molière's. 'Everything's going fine, very well indeed. Except that I can't go any faster.'

"He was riding at 25 kilometres per hour [about 15 miles per hour] and the others at 35. Gachon and the Canadian officials who surrounded him must surely have known that he couldn't ride faster than 25 while all the European riders exceeded 30. His place in the race should have been left to the American, Magnani, who is far better."

L'Auto reported with heavy irony that a rescue team sent to find Gachon spotted a cyclist heading for Le Havre at "a record speed of 18 kilometres per hour, asking in every town if anyone knew the times of liners back across the Atlantic."

The American, Magnani, that *Miroir des Sports* favored is a forgotten star of US history: the first American road international, a man who could have beaten Jonathan Boyer in being first American to ride the Tour. He won single-day races, he came ninth in Paris–Nice and he rode for America in the world road championship and came seventh, better than Fausto Coppi, who dropped out because of the heat. It was the best US performance for 33 years.

Joe Magnani's family emigrated from Italy to the coal-mining town of LaSalle, in central Illinois. He was born on July 15, 1911. That made him sixteen in 1928 when his father fell ill from working in the mines. The family had eight children. Food would go further in fewer mouths so his parents sent him and his elder sister, Angelina, to live with members of the family near Nice in southeast France. Joe joined a cycling club there, started racing and at 22 won a race put on by his club's sponsor, the 1934 GP Urago. He turned professional for Urago next year and received a license signed by Frank Kramer. Things went well. He broke away in Marseille–Nice and won after seven hours. In 1938 he finished ninth in Paris–Nice. He won Marseilles–Toulon in rain so bad that only four of the eighty starters finished. He also won the two-day Circuit of Lourdes through the Pyrenees.

In 1939, he joined another French team, Terrot, and won the first stage of the Tour of Southeast France. And then Germany invaded Poland. World war two began. Magnani won a stage of the GP Côte d'Azur, a stage of the Circuit du Mont Ventoux, and came tenth in the Grand Prix des Nations, considered the world time-trial championship. He also married his French fiancée, Mimi.

But risks were rising. Japan, Germany and Italy went to war against the USA in December, 1941, and Magnani became an enemy alien. He was safe enough in unoccupied southern France to continue racing. He came second behind Victor Cosson in the Quatre Jours de la Route organized by the *Petit Dauphinois* in 1942. But Allied troops invaded North Africa that November and the Germans moved into southern France as well. They caught him in February, 1943, and put him in a camp in the north. He stayed there until French and American troops liberated Paris in August, 1944.

Magnani raced again, including the Giro d'Italia, riding for a bike company run by Giuseppe Olmo, whom Jacques Goddet saw win a gold medal at the Los Angeles Olympics. Magnani fell on the first stage and abandoned. He did, though, become first American to ride one of the three big international stage races.

In 1947, now 35, he rode the world championship in Reims, France. Only seven of the thirty-one starters finished, the fewest ever in a world championship. Magnani was among them, seventh. He rode the world championship again in 1946 and 1947 but didn't finish. He rode briefly for Tebag in 1948 and then returned to the USA. George Mount came sixth in the Olympic road race in 1976 and returned a hero. Magnani came back an unknown. He tried six-day racing, all there was to ride, but it was far different from the road. Too different. He dropped out of racing and worked for Schwinn, putting components on frames.

He died in Chicago on November 30, 1975, after a neural infection which made movement difficult. Not until five years later did Jonathan Boyer improve on his world championship placing, coming fifth at Sallanches, not far from his home in eastern France, on a day as cold and wet as Reims had been hot and dusty.

3

The People's Race

The impact of world war one in France can't be overestimated. You see it in memorials in every village—every commune but two, in fact—long lists of the dead from a few streets and fields. It was a French war, fought in France, led by the French, with more French dead than the other allied nations combined. France lost 1,322,000 men, a quarter under twenty-four. Three million more were wounded. France at the start of the second war had only half the nineteen- to twenty-one-year-olds it would have had without the War To End All Wars.

Robert Cole, professor of European history at Utah State University, says: "The slaughter of those four years and the horrors of life in the trenches produced a disillusioned and pacifist generation. Even the most patriotic of returning soldiers were fervent partisans of peace at any price. Pessimism and malaise: these were the war's legacy."

Malaise and resentment voted in a Nationalist-Catholic alliance of big business and religion which intended to rebuild a wrecked country and make Germany pay. While that looked likely, life remained quiet. When Germany couldn't or wouldn't pay, the franc fell. And then the distant storm of the New York stock market crash washed waves over France. Germany went to the right, France to the left. Not immediately or in even steps, of course, but by 1936 France had its first left-wing government. A national strike began when the far left interpreted victory as a workers' rebellion. It wasn't. But it did bring the French two weeks' paid vacation a year. And it brought them beside the road to see the Tour.

There are years that embed themselves into the folklore of nations and 1936 is one of those years in France. It was a summer, people remember, when the sun did nothing but shine, the birds sang, the sea refreshed, the wine was good. It was the start of the Good Times. In fact, for France in the Tour it was the start of the Bad Times. France

won the Tour only intermittently for the next twenty years. But since
the advent of national teams in 1930, French riders had won five times
in a row and another would win in 1937.

The Tour had become the people's race. The Left, a combination of
socialists and communists, had won paid vacations. "It was by bicycle,"
say Jean-Luc Boeuf and Yves Léonard, "that the first beneficiaries took
possession of France, spreading a great vision both democratic and
festive of their country." The communist daily, *L'Humanité*, didn't hold
back in taking the credit: from "the tight ranks of the compact mass
that lined the road rose the cries: 'Vive *L'Humanité*!'"

Few riders hinted which way they leaned. The most popular rider
in France did, though. René Vietto was brush-topped, rarely happy,
polishing his humble beginnings by insisting he had been a bellhop at
the Hotel Majestic in Cannes. The story was so appealing, a small boy
making a path through life after the rich flicked cigar ash on his shoulders, that it became truth. It remained truth even after the reporter
Gaston Benac, creator of the Grand Prix des Nations, established that
Vietto had probably never set foot in the place, still less worked there.

Vietto said as an old man that he had suicidal leanings all his life.
There were many prepared to do the job for him. The Dutch historian,
Benjo Maso, wrote: "Barely anyone within cycling had any time for
him, from the mechanics to the soigneurs, who so often got the blame
for his defeats, to his colleagues who couldn't stand the 'I'm a star' airs
that his record didn't support."

In 1934 Vietto was close to winning the Tour when duty made him
stop in the mountains, his strength, and hand a wheel to the leader, Antonin Magne. Next day trouble halted Magne again and Vietto turned
back down a mountain for 500 metres to rescue his leader once more.
If ever a story demonstrated the sacrifice of workers for the profit of
bosses, this did. France turned on Magne for exploiting his young and
sad-looking helper. "For my country, I did what I could," Vietto told
reporters. It helped that he was openly communist, a supporter if not
a member. *L'Humanité* referred to him as "our comrade".

Not that that discouraged him from acting the capitalist. His legend
as the boy who stood on the burning deck made him a draw for criteriums and track races for which he was paid beyond his talent. Like
other riders later, he entrusted his money not to a sober banker who
promised small but realizable results but to a big talker who could

beat the market. His choice was André Trialoux, the commissaire who provoked Henri Pélissier to abandon the Tour and the manager in whose arms Vietto wept for the cameras after losing. Within a few years, Trialoux had lost the lot.

Desgrange "could justifiably be called a tyrant," said Pierre Chany. His command of the Tour had become virtual command of French cycling; the Tour didn't have the all-dominating status that it has now but Desgrange controlled dozens of riders' seasons and ambitions because he and he alone chose who from France would ride. And only he decided which foreign nations. And only he decided where the race would go, how it would be run, how long the stages would be and how many he would hold.

He was a terrifying figure to many, omnipotent, and yet he had a mischievous side even if it was at the expense of others. He fell out once with Émile Mercier, a provincial bike-maker later to sponsor Raymond Poulidor. André Leducq, he of the Lucky Strikes, had asked Alcyon for another 200 francs in pay. Gentil refused and Leducq stomped off to join Mercier's new team, run by Francis Pélissier. Gentil took revenge by pushing Desgrange into leaving Leducq out of the national team in 1934, something Desgrange was happy to do to spite a Pélissier.

Mercier was annoyed. He had spent a lot of money on Leducq and he complained. Did Desgrange care? No. He had taken a decision and that was correct, final and indisputable. Mercier wrote complaint after complaint and got lawyers to write still more. Desgrange ordered his staff never to mention Mercier's name.

The trouble was that Mercier was a sponsor and a bike-maker and sometimes had to have his complaints published. L'Auto compromised by never spelling his name correctly. That drove Mercier to still deeper fury. L'Auto then printed corrections, only to get the name wrong once more. "Monsieur Gercier has let us know that his name is Monsieur Mervier", and a few editions later, "Monsieur Mervier asks us to say that, in reality, he is called Monsieur Cermier." When the nonexistent Monsieur Cermier wrote in, L'Auto excelled itself by printing: "Monsieur Cermier insists that in fact he is known as Monsieur Merdier".

"Merde", put politely, is French for excrement.

Who won? Mercier by a technical knockout. He arranged to make Leducq correspondent of L'Auto's rival, Paris-Soir, following the Tour from which he was banished as a rider and, what's more, writing for an evening paper which printed Tour news the day that it happened and not, like *L'Auto*, the day after. Desgrange had to run all the stages later in the day to stop it.

Desgrange married and soon divorced. Only one woman loved him for long and that was an avant-garde artist, Jane Deley. She wouldn't marry him because she didn't want to give up her name and she once referred to Desgrange as Monsieur Deley.

Deley was born Jeanne—it was as Jean, more usually a male name, that she signed her works—in Creusot, in eastern central France, on July 28, 1878. She and Desgrange met some time after world war one. They made an odd couple, Desgrange rigid and formal, Deley moving in a world of bohemians and creatives. It's probable she had had affairs with some of them. Desgrange liked her friends even though he may not have understood them and began a paper called *Comœdia*, which carried news of the entertainment world in the way *L'Auto* printed sport. It failed. There wasn't enough news and impresarios saw no reason to advertise if the paper didn't promise uncritical coverage.

Deley pushed Desgrange into buying a château of arcades and courtyards and flamboyance on the road to St-Maxime, across the bay from an unknown village called St-Tropez. The building had changed hands several times and the last owners wanted to turn it into a casino. Desgrange and Deley bought it cheap when the council refused. It was there Desgrange retired after insisting on starting the Tour of 1936. Prostate operations, these days straightforward, were then in two parts. The first had been completed but not the second. Desgrange fitted his car with cushions and softened suspension. He rode with a nurse at his side. And then he handed over, if that's the word for a man who could barely mumble, control to Goddet.

Desgrange ran a couple of hours a day all his life. During the Tour he clambered for an hour on the steep shingle beds under ski lifts. On a rest day at Perpignan he ran twelve kilometres from Le Castillet to Canet-Plage. The heavy-drinking, exercise-resistant Albert Baker d'Isy, joint founder of the Grand Prix des Nations, recounted that "his great joy was to drag along the secretary-general of the Tour, Lucien Cazalis, who didn't have the same talent and followed him sweating and panting." Jacques Goddet said everybody made himself scarce whenever Desgrange looked for his running shoes. Even dying in his villa, he shuffled across his room with a stopwatch to measure how he was holding off the Grim Reaper. He died on August 16, 1940, Deley nine years later.

Jacques Goddet always wondered how life would have been had Desgrange had a son. Desgrange treated him as the son he never had, called him "*mon petit Jacques*" and showed little doubt that he would join the business. The two resembled each other. They were of their era, of course, Desgrange formed by the shame of defeat, Goddet more easygoing. But Goddet, too, believed in sport shaping men. Like Pierre de Coubertin, one of Desgrange's contemporaries (although Desgrange never believed de Coubertin was right to be obsessed with amateurism), Goddet was impressed by English private schools. De Coubertin had seen how sport was institutionalized at Rugby, the school which gave the sport of the same name and, less flatteringly, an image of bullying in *Tom Brown's Schooldays*. De Coubertin believed the sport of British private schools—which provided Britain's politicians, generals and businessmen—created the nation's "moral and social strength." Goddet followed a similar path and came to the same conclusion.

Goddet hadn't been a wonderful student at St-Marie-de-Monceau in Paris. War interrupted his lessons, air raids and shelling sending his family into the cellars at 20 bis, rue de la Boétie, off the boulevard Haussmann. His parents separated at the start of the 1920s and, perhaps to avoid choosing with which he would live, he asked to go to school in England. His parents weren't sure. He wouldn't pass his baccalaureate, proving stone of a French education. But at sixteen Goddet turned up at Courtenay Lodge College on the Thames in the fourteenth-century village of Sutton Courtenay. He remembered: "At the weekend, the tradition was to go to Oxford, about fifteen kilometres away, and we went by bicycle. My schoolboy friends rode solid roadster bikes, big saddle and wide, straight handlebars. I stood out by having a racing bike sent from France, a La Française-Diamant with cable brakes that astonished the others. With that advantage, I had no trouble riding away from them."

He remembered morning lessons, afternoon games, then more classes. His favorites were rugby and tennis, reaching the college final in tennis but breaking his arm at rugby. It didn't put him off "the healthy and beneficial logic of British education, which allowed pupils every day of the week to make the most of a ball or to practice some other sport without reducing the time for class work." If only France had the sense to do things the same way.

He followed his first Tour, or enough to have an understanding, in 1928. He took the overnight train and joined the race as it rode from La Rochelle to Sables-d'Olonne. He followed, too, over cols he described as "earth paths, muddy, stony", seeing the race leave Bayonne in darkness to have the sixteen hours to finish the stage.

Where Goddet differed from Desgrange is that, while honoring traditions, he hadn't invented them. He quickly allowed derailleur gears, for instance, banned by Desgrange because they falsified the difference between men. And a social shakeup almost as great as Dreyfus but longer lasting and more constructive was to make him accept the Tour de France as a show as much as a sport.

4
Tour Of Dreams

The problem cited now is that national teams brought together riders whose interests lay elsewhere. Would a Belgian ride against a Frenchman who normally employed him? Would yearlong rivals in the same team ride for or against each other? Fausto Coppi and Gino Bartali ruined their chances in the 1949 world championship in Holland rather than see the other win. France went further: Jacques Anquetil refused to ride if Louison Bobet or Raymond Poulidor threatened his leadership.

And yet before 1930 people were complaining the opposite. Goddet spotted that "riders of the same nationality but belonging to two different teams, driven on by an ever-growing band of following journalists, cultivated a noticeable chauvinism, coming to arrangements between themselves."

France was delighted with the first Tour in national colors. A Frenchman won—André Leducq—and a French dreamboat took eight stages, with seven second places and eighteen finishes in the first three. It's never been equaled. Charles Pélissier was a brother apart. Francis was blunt and Henri bloody-minded. But Charles was Valentino, a charmer and seducer. He looked sleek, his face unlined, his mouth wide and his eyes dark-lined and powerful. His conquests, it seems possible, included Desgrange's ladyfriend, Jane. Desgrange probably didn't know; if he had, he might not have been such a *Charlot* fan. Or maybe he just forgave everything because at last a Pélissier had done his race honor.

What made events more exciting is that he had a rival for wins and women. Even if you don't know him, you'll know the tradition he brought about. Because Raffaele Di Paco, in the 1935 Giro d'Italia, was the first rider to have his name painted on the road. Nowadays any Tom or Dick gets his name on the mountains. You can paint your own. Nobody will stop you. But Di Paco was first. Why? Because he was the original Mario Cipollini, a sprinter as flashy off his bike as on it. An Italian journalist said he'd have no trouble listing Di Paco's wins and those of riders he'd beaten to get them. "But," he smirked, "I wouldn't even get part way through the virgins and impressionable young women he managed to deflower."

Di Paco was handsome, the right height, well built without being a strongman, with a smile that lit his face. His hair was lightly oiled and brushed up and back with a matinée idol parting. This dark-haired handsome man won fifteen stages of the Giro and nine of the Tour de France. "You want to finish second?" team managers used to tell their riders. "Pick his wheel in the sprint."

Italy preferred immaculate brutes dashing for the line to emaciated climbers pedaling through mist. Di Paco was the most immaculate brute of all. But in 1931 he heard that Desgrange insisted he was in the Italian team for the Tour. He received the news with sadness. He lived the cold-sweat nightmare of the road coiling endlessly above him. To quit with a trade team would bring shame and a cut in wages but not the humiliation and ridicule of pulling out with an Italian jersey over his shoulders.

The Italians went by sleeper to Paris. Legend says Di Paco packed a case big enough only for cycling shoes, pajamas and a toothbrush. His race jersey, shorts and yellow bike with two metal bidons would be provided by the Tour. He left home, however, with two cases: the little one and one much larger. In that he had packed suit, shirts and shoes. He gave it to the railroad company to ship to Paris to collect after the race. That way, to abandon in the mountains would mean crossing France in race clothes or pajamas. No Italian seducer was going to sit in a train in his pajamas.

(It ought to be true. It does overlook, though, that he would have had the clothes in which he went to Paris.)

In 1931, he was in yellow after stage four. A day later he was still leader but level with Pélissier. They posed for photos but their reputations and their sprinting were too alike. At Charleroi they started swinging punches. And then came the mountains. Di Paco had a hellish time. We know that because everybody did. Karel Steyaert called his paper the night after the Tourmalet and dictated: "What happy people are the Chinese, never having heard of the Tour de France."

Jef Demuysère, Alfons Schepers and Félicien Vervaecke chose that day to rid the Tour of the French. They attacked on the Tourmalet and took only Di Paco's teammate, Antonio Pesenti. The four looked as though they would share the stage and the Tour. And then came the misery of Steyaert's line to *Sportwereld*. The Tour was about to be a Belgian benefit when each Belgian in turn flatted. Forced to replace their tires and then inflate them, they were caught by the French leader, Magne, who dropped to Luchon delighted at the Belgian distress and won by five minutes. With the three minutes' bonus Desgrange offered to discourage sprints, he won the Tour.

And Di Paco? He finished almost an hour and a half adrift, last but five. His fears had come true. It had a cathartic effect, though. He got going and even won lesser stages in the Pyrenees and the Alps. Luchon–Perpignan, for instance, took in the Portet d'Aspet and the Puymorens and he won that after twelve and a half hours. Between Évian and Belfort, with the Faucille at 1,320 metres, he broke away with Ludwig Geyer of Germany and won by 6 minutes, 24 seconds over the third man, Gaston Rebry. His loss by the *Parc des Princes* was 2 hours, 11 minutes, 11 seconds, most of it from the Tourmalet. He came seventeenth, having won five stages. Next year he finished thirty-third and again avoided traveling home in pajamas. He died on May 21, 1996, in the Tuscan villa in which he'd been born. Remember him next time you see riders' names on the road.

These were great years for the Tour, wonderful summers for France. Desgrange painted French teams that traded stages and victories between themselves as bands of friends, *bandes de copains*. The rest of the press joined in, promoting the romance of cycling in Hollywood star-factory conspiracy. Sure, the riders posed together and on the road they worked together. But Pélissier and Leducq didn't get on, forced by commercial circumstances to ride together in six-days but trying not to speak otherwise, on top of which Leducq was the better rider but the more glamorous Pélissier was paid half again as much in criteriums; Magne was a cold loner who barely spoke and withdrew into himself when anyone tried to make him; Georges Speicher was too prone to being a party boy—he was boogying in a nightclub when France named him at the last moment for the 1933 world championship, which he then won—and Maurice Archambaud was simply thickheaded.

But no matter: the Tour had become more than a race. It was a show, and like all shows it was part glamour and part reality. Joséphine Baker, she of sexy stage dances dressed in little but bananas, kissed the riders *bonne route* in 1933 and the crowd loved it. So many turned up that police closed the road for the entire race, the first time it happened.

When in 1934 René Vietto sacrificed his chances by handing his wheel to Magne in the mountains, France was delirious. There was no television and little honesty. Vietto said at the time he had done it for his country. Later he was more honest: it had been *un holdup,* a robbery, an act forced on him. That was why he wept by the roadside, seated on a wall with his one-wheeled bicycle beside him. The emotion was increased by the way the photo was cropped: the crowd with him was cut away to exaggerate the distress of a man alone with his misery.

Vietto's discontent at being halted where he was strongest, on the climbs, was the more acute because Desgrange had gone back on generous bonuses for sprinters and offered them to climbers. That way Desgrange got a better show, more battling with destiny and gravity, while keeping in the race featherweight climbers who got up mountains fast but rarely excelled going back down them.

The Tour had evolved. The mountains for two decades were places merely to survive. It was enough to get up them. That they were regarded as superhuman challenges shows in the way Gustave Garrigou won five sovereigns for riding the Tourmalet without putting his foot to the ground. Now there were gifted climbers, men like Vietto who could race in the mountains rather than struggle.

This was recognized in 1934, the year Vietto abandoned his chances (as France saw it, of winning the Tour, as Vietto saw it, of winning in the mountains), by a new Grand Prix de la Montagne. Evolution took care of it in two ways. Evolution because riders were better, evolution because Menier, the chocolate company, was so delighted by reaction to prizes it gave at mountain tops that it sponsored an entire competition. There would now be a race within a race, not for the yellow jersey of leadership—though that remained the goal of every rider—but to show best over the Ballon d'Alsace, Galibier, Vars, Allos, Braus, Peyresourde, Aspin, Tourmalet and Aubisque.

Steadily, the Tour was changing in other ways. The *touristes-routiers* such as Jules Banino had become *isolés* and then individuals, and were now, well, still what they were but looked after by the Tour in the same way as the big riders. There was an aberration in 1935 when Desgrange allowed teams which had lost riders to recruit replacements from among them but the times were changing.

The Tour was more and more decided in the mountains. The individuals were grouped into secondary teams such as Cadets de France and Bleuets (1938) and Belgium B (1939), and into regional teams (also 1939) representing the west, southwest, southeast and the north of France, although who went into which often had little link with where they lived or had been born.

Regional teams may have been makeweights, intended to mop up good riders who hadn't made better teams, but they had a disproportionate effect. Benjo Maso said they "gave the Tour a separate character. Almost every day the battle broke out right after the start and because none of the 'A' teams was in condition or prepared to control the race properly, anarchy broke out in which attacks came one after the other at high speed. That was a fundamental difference from the Giro. That was run with trade teams in which the leaders exercised strict discipline. Attacks could be made only when the team leader or the manager said so. And when a breakaway got clear the riders rarely worked together well. There were almost always riders in the group who'd been ordered to save themselves or not to take part. The result was that barely anything happened in most stages of the Tour of Italy and the only full-out racing was in the three or four mountain stages.

"It was no wonder, therefore, that Italian riders who had come to France with Bartali and Ronconi had so much trouble with the high speed and the constant changes of tempo from the first stages."

The system was just perfecting itself when Italy pulled out, condemned by the world for invading Ethiopia. Spain stayed at home ruined by the civil war. And Germany, with things on its mind larger than the Tour de France, invaded Poland.

5
The Enigma of 1940

Maurice Goddet was a party animal, the largest shareholder in *L'Auto*. When *L'Auto* stopped him spending its money—its finances were never secure—he went on splashing his own. By 1938 he had run out and he sold his shares to make ends meet. This may seem unimportant, not to mention dull. But it came close to branding his brother a Nazi collaborationist and even a war criminal.

Maurice Goddet sold his interests to Raymond Patenôtre, a 39-year-old press baron who lived in an impressive mansion he had designed himself in the rue de la Faisanderie. His business manager was Albert Lejeune, the founder of Paris–Nice in 1933 and director of *Le Petit Journal* and *Le Petit Niçois*, two prominent dailies. He came to a sticky end, shot in Marseille in January 1945 as a collaborator. Why? Because at the start of the war Patenôtre fled to the USA, where he had been born in Atlantic City in the summer of 1900. He left his business interests to Lejeune. But Lejeune had been collaborating with the *Propaganda Abteilung*, which supervised the press and encouraged collaboration. He sold it Patenôtre's shares and *L'Auto* passed into German control.

The early days of the war had seen the paper in even greater money trouble. There were few sports events and the nation's athletes were at war. To fill columns and increase sales, *L'Auto* began printing general news in a column headed "*Savoir Vite*", or "news in brief." Goddet said: "I found myself obliged to keep this wretched column under the Occupation just to keep the right to publish! It contained war communiqués from the Occupants which, apart from being obligatory, were printed under the heading of non-sporting news, which gave the impression that we had published it ourselves."

At the end of the war, the government closed *L'Auto* as collaborationist, nailing planks across its door. Its belongings were sequestrated

and Goddet called to an inquiry. His position wasn't straightforward. For a start, he was a supporter of Philippe Pétain—the hero of
Verdun in the first war—to whom France had turned in defeat, for
want of anyone more charismatic. He printed editorials in Pétain's
favor even as the old soldier abandoned democracy and suspended
the French Republic. "In 1940, France started another life," Goddet
wrote in November of that year. "The Marshal is going to give it a
purifying bath."

Émile Besson, who followed the Tour for *L'Humanité* for 35 years,
said: "The two points are that, first, Jacques Goddet in what he wrote
was a longtime supporter of Marshal Pétain. He wrote prudently but
he did it nevertheless. The second is that *L'Auto* scrupulously published
all the Nazi propaganda communiqués."

It was not against the law to be a Pétain supporter. It was the mark
of a man of the right to remain one, as Pétain became more and more
a German puppet. But in the strictest sense, that was loyalty rather
than treason. Goddet said in his biography that he couldn't shut shop,
closing the paper rather than collaborate, because other people's living
depended on it. Pierre Chany, who worked alongside him for decades
after the war, said: "Jacques Goddet never sold anyone. Jacques Goddet, during the war, looked after the business, kept the shop running.
In a way, yes, he was passive concerning the Occupant. But that was no
more than 98 percent of the population in 1940."

What is less straightforward is Goddet's role in Operation Spring
Wind. At dawn on July 16, 1942, French police and German soldiers
rounded up 13,000 Jews in Paris and incarcerated 7,000 of them in
the *Vélodrome d'Hiver*, the indoor bike track close to the Eiffel Tower.
There they were locked in, the windows, doors and five of the ten lava-
tories nailed shut. The glass roof, painted blue to prevent reflections
which could guide bombers, made the heat intolerable. They had only
one water faucet among them, says the writer Jon Henley. The only
food and extra water for five days was brought by Quakers.

The Quakers took out letters the Jews had written. In one, a young
mother called Paulette Stokfisz-Bronstein wrote: "The police came and
arrested all the Jews in the building, they took me and my two children,
I am writing to say we are being taken to the *Vélodrome d'Hiver*. I ask
you to go to my home, 1 passage du Jeu-de-Boules in the eleventhth
[arrondissement of Paris], to get the keys from the concierge. Just take

all that's there. Take all my things, all you find…Bring me a few jars of conserves and two skirts so I can change." She had no reply.

The Jews were taken from the *Vel' d'Hiv'* to a holding camp just outside the city, in a block of unfinished apartments at Drancy, or to open-air camps elsewhere. Paulette went to Pithiviers transit camp, in the countryside to the south. Without a reply from other letters, she wrote again: "I am perhaps leaving again for an unknown destination. My cousin has already left, her son stayed behind but he is with me. I am going to leave. Jacques and Raymonde [her children] will be left alone. The Red Cross may ask you to take them in. I beg you Nana, accept…Jacques can look after himself. Raymonde goes to school. They won't bother you. Dear Nana, go to my flat and take everything, I give it all to you. I will send you a parcel. There is some money and my jewels. Keep them…I beg you, have pity on my children. I think this is my last letter…Keep all I asked you to send. I don't need anything any more."

LES 16 ET 17 JUILLET 1942
13152 JUIFS FURENT ARRETES DANS PARIS ET SA BANLIEUE
DEPORTES ET ASSASSINES A AUSCHWITZ.
DANS LE VELODROME D'HIVER QUI S'ELEVAIT ICI
4115 ENFANTS
2916 FEMMES
1129 HOMMES
FURENT PARQUES DANS DES CONDITIONS INHUMAINES
PAR LA POLICE DU GOUVERNEMENT DE VICHY,
SUR ORDRE DES OCCUPANTS NAZIS.
QUE CEUX QUI ONT TENTE DE LEUR VENIR EN AIDE
SOIENT REMERCIES.
PASSANT, SOUVIENS-TOI !

The track that died of shame. At the foot of an ugly apartment block near the Eiffel Tower stands a memorial to Jews interned in the Vel' d'Hiv' and then sent for extermination. The question: what was Jacques Goddet's role?

Paulette was sent to Auschwitz on August 7. Her children, Jacques and Raymonde, followed on September 2. Neither they nor most of the others, including all the children, came back.

The *Vel' d'Hiv'* belonged to Goddet. It was he who gave the keys to the Germans. It's possible he did it at gunpoint. What is intriguing is that he made so little of it in his autobiography. There are theories about moving Israel to the Australian desert, lists of cars in his paper's races and rallies, even accounts of schoolday bike rides. But the keys of the *Vel' d'Hiv'* get just a few words. Why, if he was forced to hand them over? Would an explanation not have made an ambiguous position clearer? And what, therefore, does it mean that he says so little?

There are pages of justification about his wartime activities. There's emphasis that he refused to run the Tour when the Germans asked and there's condemnation of his former colleague, Jean Leulliot (successor to Lejeune as organizer of Paris–Nice), for holding such a race instead. Whether Goddet printed German news in his paper isn't much compared to the slaughter of the *Vel' d'Hiv'*.

In 1945, as a *résistant de la dernière heure*—someone who joined the Resistance when victory was assured—Goddet joined an assault on a Parisian ministry occupied by the Germans. At the inquiry, he could point to that, and he could insist he had no choice but print German news. He could say he had brought Patrice Thominet, an active resistant, into the paper's management. It appears Goddet didn't know his printers, under Roger Roux, the print room manager, were printing Resistance pamphlets and Charles de Gaulle's speeches, but that didn't harm his cause either. The inquiry concluded he had been a Pétainist but that neither he nor his paper had been ultra-collaborators.

The government wasn't, however, going to give him the Tour. For that, he would have to fight. He could start another paper, on condition it wasn't called *L'Auto*, that it wasn't on yellow paper, that he wasn't named as author—considered unfair competition for other fledgling papers—and that for a while he couldn't even enter the building. The paper, published from a building rented from the sequestrated *L'Auto* and on the opposite side of the road, was named *L'Équipe*. Goddet said the name—"the team"—symbolized how France would recover from war.

The communists—once the Soviet Union had neutrality attacked out of it—were the driving force of the Resistance. They were a political force as well. Communist sympathizers had press interests beyond *L'Humanité* and, through two magazines, *Sports* and *Miroir Sprint*, applied to run the Tour. De Gaulle wouldn't countenance a French monument falling to communists but there was no credible competition. Goddet was innocent but not as innocent as all that.

How it happened isn't clear, but Goddet became associated with Émilien Amaury, a left-winger who had used his job with Pétain's government at Vichy to procure paper and other material for the Resistance. Amaury was a resistant from the start, an early recruit for the rue de Lille group, one of several in Paris which printed clandestine newspapers. It was through that that Amaury may have known Roger Roux in *L'Auto*'s press room, and through *L'Auto* he knew Goddet. Amaury was a stainless man to have on your side.

Amaury had ambitions. He had become a major shareholder in a Parisian daily, *Le Parisien Libéré,* itself revived from a paper closed after the war. It's hard to think he hadn't looked at *L'Équipe* with greed in his eyes. He and Goddet formed the *Société du Stade-Vélodrome du Parc des Princes*, in which they were equal shareholders. They and the communist bidders each ran trial races, Amaury and Goddet's clearly better. Amaury thereby became joint owner of the Tour.

Besson, *L'Humanite*'s man and a Resistant from when he was seventeen, called the victory political, which suggests de Gaulle told his advisors not to pick communists. "After the Liberation, the battle between Left and Right had the Tour as one of its prizes. It was a bit much to have given them the right to run the Tour again after all that," he said, referring to the *Vel' d'Hiv'* and German propaganda.

Amaury imposed his control on the Tour. Goddet could look after traditions and the race, but business was to be left to Félix Lévitan, his head of sport at *Le Parisien Libéré,* whom he made Goddet's partner. From then until 1965 publicity for the Tour had the logos of both *L'Équipe* and *Le Parisien Libéré.* In 1965 Goddet's son died in a car crash and Goddet ceded his shares in *L'Équipe* and the Tour to Amaury. The Tour is now run by the Amaury Sport Organisation.

Goddet, everyone will tell you, was no easy touch round the office but he was a gentleman. Amaury rarely was. He moved to the right and was at the center of the longest printers' strike in France. He was so disliked that the left-leaning *Libération* reported his death with the headline: "Amaury falls from horse: horse is safe."

Part four: La Chasse

The "échappée matinale" may get a great distance or it may spend hours with only a minute's advantage. The trick for the others is not to catch the leaders too soon, for then other attacks will arise and more energy will be spent on chasing anew, nor to leave it so long that the leaders cross the line before they are caught. They must be decide when to take up "la chasse", the hunt.

1

Out Of The Shadows

Professional cyclists—those we know of—rarely distinguished themselves in the war. Jean Robic, a goblin Frenchman whose legs and courage made up for his mouth and personality, carried messages for the Resistance. Louis Bobet—he hadn't yet acquired the diminutive, Louison—kept a determined distance from profiteering. But, according to Émile Besson, he was a rarity; many were too busy racing and dabbling in the black market to end the war honorably.

"You know any other riders [than Bobet] who resisted?" he asked. "I'll tell you: under the Occupation, riders almost all took part in the black market. They sprinted like trash collectors for eggs, hams and sausage which then they rushed off to sell." He overlooked the minor role of Jean Robic but otherwise there aren't stories to contradict him.

In Holland, police caught Wim van Est leading cows across from Belgium at night. He said: "I told the court it was dark, that I found this rope and I was amazed it had cows on the end of it." That was immediately after the war. Van Est—Holland's first *maillot jaune*—was one of fourteen children. He winked about whether the cows had been his first brush with the illegal. His uncle, Wout Wagtmans, "wasn't nicknamed 'Smuggler' for nothing," he said. "Who wasn't a smuggler?"

As a side note, Jacques Anquetil, the first man to win the Tour five times, is always described as the son of a strawberry farmer. But he wasn't. Anquetil's father, when Jacques was born, was a builder. When the Germans insisted he work on the Atlantic Wall, he refused and lost his business as a result. It was then, the price of resistance, that he became a strawberry cropper.

Albert Lejeune, founder of Paris–Nice, was executed for collaboration. His successor, Jean Leulliot, left *L'Auto* for the ultra-collaborationist *France Socialiste*. He promoted an ersatz Tour, the Circuit de France.

It ran from September 28 to October 4, 1942, starting and finishing in Paris, passing through Le Mans, Poitiers, Limoges, Clermont-Ferrand, St-Étienne, Lyon and Dijon. It needed German cooperation to cross from the occupied north to the nominally independent south. The president, Pierre Laval, greeted riders and congratulated organizers at St-Étienne. He was shot as a collaborator in October, 1945.

Leulliot also came close to being found guilty. Only the appeals of journalists saved him. Perhaps they thought he was naive. Maybe he had suffered enough. The race was a disaster. The distances were wildly out and the race ran behind schedule. Riders became lost in the mountains of the Auvergne as night fell. Louis Caput, later Raymond Poulidor's manager, was alone in half-darkness with not even a following car when, with twenty kilometres to go, he saw a man waving a handkerchief. It was the only way an official had to show that, there in the middle of nowhere, the stage was to finish rather than enter Clermont-Ferrand at night.

Goddet wrote: "Do you understand, Jean, up there above us, why I have never since shown any bitterness towards you? This shameless demonstration was enough to stop the attempt ever being repeated. This 'great first' Circuit de France has remained...the only one."

The Tour of Flanders was no more scrupulous, the only classic run in Occupied Europe. The organizer, Karel Steyaert (also known as Karel van Wijnendaele), asked the Germans for the go-ahead. They wanted a wartime Tour to suggest things were close to normal in France, that the occupation was permanent. That was why they approved a Tour of Flanders in Belgium. Gabe Konrad, editor of *On the Wheel*, said the Germans "not only allowed and enjoyed the race but helped police the route as well."

Steyaert's newspapers, *De Standaard* and *Het Algemeen Nieuws*, were confiscated by the state just as *L'Auto* had been. Steyaert was forbidden ever to work as a journalist, a ban he escaped thanks to a letter from the British general, Bernard Montgomery, confirming he had hidden British pilots.

The difference between the second war and the first is that fewer continental Europeans, and therefore cyclists, fought in it. Every nation the Germans invaded, save the Soviet Union, was overwhelmed within days, weeks at best. The first war took a greater slaughter. The fact that later cyclists collaborated or at any rate profited could be no more than that they had the chance. Others were honest, upright and brave. But of those we don't hear. And just a few, like Roger Lévêque, survived concentration camps, taking the yellow jersey in the Tour of 1951.

The Germans came close to Paris in the first war. The French pushed them back north, going into battle in Paris taxis, and the war stagnated into trench fighting. French casualties were far higher than in 1939–45 but devastation was restricted to an area which journalists investigating the revival of Paris–Roubaix called "the hell of the north."

The second war was the reverse, many fewer Frenchmen fighting and their battle ending in 1940. The wreckage, however, was more widespread. France had to pay for the right to be occupied. War production was for German benefit and machinery and other goods were taken across the border. The railroad network, crucial to the economy, was wrecked by bombing. So was heavy industry. An unusually cold winter halted agriculture.

In 1947 George Marshall, the American secretary of state, told graduates at Harvard: "It is logical that the United States should do whatever it is able to do to assist in the return of normal economic health to the world, without which there can be no political stability and no assured peace." In a hotel around the corner from the American embassy in Paris—a plaque marks the spot—the USA and western Europe agreed to $12 billion in return for opening Europe to American goods. Of that, France received $2,296 million, second only to the United Kingdom's $3,297 million.

The Tour did not wait for Marshall Aid. Its revival contrasted to the state of the country and the privations of its people. Ration coupons in the last years of the war were futile because there was nothing to buy. The bread allowance in summer 1947, two years after Liberation, was 200 grams a day, seven ounces, lower than through the occupation. The franc slid. Imports dried up. Government planners told Goddet to go away when he asked to run a Tour in 1946. When he returned for 1947, France needed something lift the gloom and legend says dock workers threatened to strike if they weren't given their race. That may be apocryphal; what is true is that Goddet knew his link with Amaury and *Le Parisien Libéré* strengthened his negotiations with the government. It's hard to think the point was missed when the two men discussed their partnership.

They dealt with Maurice Kaouza, a young teacher from Senegal who had supported de Gaulle throughout the war. Kaouza had become a government commissaire and his smiling confidence worked wonders. Goddet, in this time of gloom and privation, needed 20,000 liters of gas (5,300 gallons), 2,200 pounds of meat, 1,500 pounds of sugar, 350 pounds of cheese, 8,000 bananas, 18,000 oranges, 12,000 loaves, 950 chickens…and nearly 800 gallons of wine. He got them. He also acquired 175 bicycles, 350 pairs of goggles, 6,000 drinking bottles and 150 suitcases. The two aluminum drinks bottles that riders received were to be handed back at the end or paid for.

Nothing was certain, though. France had nine governments between liberation and the end of 1948, no party holding a majority nor sustaining a coalition. Strikes included a shutdown of mines for eight weeks, when industry and house-heating depended on coal. Shutdowns included the post office, which troubled riders who needed passports and country boys who had to confirm their entry by telegram, probably the first they had ever sent.

And yet the Tour went ahead, a mix of old stars and new faces. Louis Aragon, director of the evening paper, *Ce Soir*, captured the atmosphere: "The Tour…It's a summer fête for men, but it's also a fête for all our country, with a passion that's singularly French: too bad for those who can't share the emotions, the follies, the hopes! I have never lost my childhood love for this grand rite that's renewed every year. But I have learned to see in it, to read in it, something else: something written in the anxious eyes of the riders, in the effort of their muscles, in the sweat and the willing pain. The lesson of national energy, the violent wish to beat nature and one's own body, the exaltation of everyone for the best. The lesson repeated every year shows that France is alive and that the Tour is above all the Tour de France."

2

The Fabulous Fifties

Jean-Paul Ollivier is a kind, gray-haired man you'd wish as an uncle. For years he worked from a small office on an upper floor of the *Télévisions France* building in the avenue Montaigne in Paris. He brushed with models and designers as he walked to work because this is the heart of the *haute couture* district. Since 1998 the state television service has moved to the suburbs, across the ring road from the headquarters of *L'Équipe* and the Tour in Issy-les-Moulineaux.

Ollivier has been broadcasting since 1964. He is a loved feature of French coverage even if there's a sense that the main commentators, who included Laurent Jalabert and the late Laurent Fignon, think him an anachronism. *Pollo-la-Science* ("Paul-Who-Knows-All") keeps his place because of his love of France, its countryside and architecture— TV regularly breaks to tell the history of châteaux and cathedrals, a good half of the audience being as interested in France from the air as in the racers—and because of his extraordinary memory for cycling's past.

And the past, he says, was never better than the Fifties. "Cycle racing was not only at its peak but it was rich with personalities. After the war, Europe was looking for its own personality. Cycling provided that. That's what the sponsors and the teams have all but killed off. And then, because Europe was moving again, there was a rivalry between nations—a good rivalry: France, Belgium, Spain, Italy, they all had their champions. Now, it's as if they come off a production line."

The base of that rivalry was the Challenge Desgrange-Colombo. It had been hard before the war to get riders and teams to other lands. Now, Europeans don't need passports. The borders are open. The currency is identical from the Arctic Circle to Athens. But then, travel was slow and difficult, borders tedious, currencies expensive to change, and few companies sold anything outside their own country. What interest did Spaniards or Italians have in France? Why would French riders race in Belgium unless they were sure of a prize?

That was the problem *L'Équipe* tackled with its counterparts in Belgium and Italy. Between them they established a competition, named after the founders of the Tour and the Giro d'Italia, to reward riders for their travel. It wasn't just for the sport, of course. There were commercial reasons. *L'Équipe, La Gazetta dello Sport, Les Sports* and *Het Nieuwsblad-Sportwereld* all organized races. All would sell more if their races became international. And readers would follow their favorites abroad and buy papers all summer.

The first races were the Tour, the Giro, Milan–San Remo, Paris–Roubaix, the Tour of Flanders, the Flèche Wallonne, Paris–Brussels and the Tour of Lombardy. The tours of Switzerland and Spain were added later.

Ollivier's "good international rivalry" wasn't always smiling. The man in yellow towards the end of the Tour in 1947 was born in France but his parents were Italian and so was their son. And Brambilla just sounds Italian. Pierre Brambilla was riding from Caen to Paris, comfortably because tradition insisted the race leader should ride the last day without aggravation. Not that tradition troubled Jean Robic. The race had just dropped into the Seine valley when he saw Brambilla surrounded by other riders, too surrounded to respond quickly to an attack.

Germany had occupied most of France but Italians had the regions around Nice, which had once been Italian. Brambilla was Italian. Brambilla was therefore fair game. Whether that was the reasoning Robic went through as he broke clear on a hill through the suburb of Bonsecours in Rouen, it occurred to everyone else. Witness after witness says Robic and another Frenchman, Edouard Fachleitner, were paced by motorcycle outriders so that they finished with thirteen minutes' lead. Riders spoke of anti-Italian atmosphere that hindered Brambilla's efforts to do anything about it. Robic won the Tour and Brambilla, legend insists, buried his bike in his garden. Two years later he took French citizenship.

What would have made the Tour truly international were Italians better than the French-Italian Brambilla or even the "real" Italians, all minor, riding with him. But the biggest names wouldn't come. Benjo Maso said: "Italy had two riders in the immediate postwar era who were head and shoulders better than the competition: Fausto Coppi and Gino Bartali. Goddet really wanted to have the battles between these superstars brought from the Giro d'Italia to the Tour. But signing on both *campionissimi* looked exceptionally difficult. First, France and Italy had accepted a peace agreement at the start of the year but it hadn't been ratified. Officially, the two countries were still at war. Under those circumstances, the Italian cycling federation didn't feel it could cooperate.

"More than that, the bike factories that employed them, Bianchi and Legnano, weren't inclined to release their highly paid stars for a month. Riders in the Tour had to ride an unlabelled yellow bike and a win would bring them little publicity. Goddet was so anxious to engage the two champions that he was prepared to make an exception, but to no avail. It was clear that Coppi and Bartali would stay home and that the UVI would send no official team to France."

Bartali rode the Tour twice before the war and then in 1948 he was persuaded to return. He was disoriented by where he was and what he was doing. The order had changed. There were *brisquards*—old lags—on the line but there were a lot of whom he had never heard. He had the numbers of those to watch taped to his handlebars but the race started in rain. Riders' waterproofs obscured the numbers and Bartali recognized barely anyone.

The attacks were instant, with the dignity of an upturned hornet nest. A rider zoomed past Bartali and the Italian clung to him, in Ollivier's words, "with the desperation of a man in a shipwreck." It turned out to be a prewar hero, Briek Schotte. The two came on to the track at Trouville after a little less than seven hours and Bartali took the Tour's first yellow jersey. The Italian press had been sniffy about the venture, seeing no need for the country's best to cross into a land known for bad breath and smelly armpits. And it was true at the time that the French bought less soap than any nation in Europe. Leading the Tour from the first day changed things, however. Bartali was an old man but there was fire in his belly. Italian fire. Italy, recovering from Mussolini and a war fought on both sides, needed fiery bellies more than most.

Such was the change Bartali brought that he led the country out of crisis. The communists were powerful in Italy. Their leader, Palmiro Togliatti, however, was a moderate who had abandoned armed struggle for democracy. That gave him enemies on the left but won him no friends on the right. Intervention by the CIA helped ensure he didn't win Italy's elections in 1948, the first since Mussolini was hanged upside down in the Piazzale Loreto in Milan. Togliatti was leaving the parliament building on July 14, 1948, when a sniper shot him three times in the neck. He fell into a coma.

Demonstrations broke out, trade unions called a national strike, communists took over factories and radio stations. The former prime minister, Giulio Andreotti, said it was exaggeration to say the country was close to civil war but the situation was bad enough that Alcide de Gasperi, a long-faced man with heavy features who was Italy's prime minister from 1945 to 1953, called Bartali as he was resting in the Tour.

July 14 is France's national day, what tourists call Bastille Day, and riders were having a day off in Cannes. Bartali and friends had been to the beach with cigarettes and a bottle of vermouth and they'd decided to go home if Togliatti died. They assumed the next stage would be their last.

De Gasperi reached Bartali at his hotel. Could he distract attention? He could. He won the next three stages and then the whole Tour, by fourteen minutes. His obituary in the *Daily Telegraph* recalled: "Just as it seemed the communists would stage a full-scale revolt, a deputy ran into the chamber shouting 'Bartali's won the Tour de France!' All differences were at once forgotten as the feuding politicians applauded and congratulated each other on a cause for such national pride. That day, with immaculate timing, Togliatti awoke from his coma on his hospital bed, inquired how the Tour was going, and recommended calm. All over the country political animosities were for the time being swept aside by the celebrations and a looming crisis was averted."

There is a final story. When Bartali reached Paris, he paraded around the *Parc des Princes*, attended a reception, went through interviews, then planned dinner at the Pied du Cochon restaurant across the road from the food market at Les Halles. It's still there, although the food market isn't. He had two bouquets. The first he wanted to lay at the statue of the Virgin Mary in Nôtre Dame and the second he hoped to place on Desgrange's grave.

Desgrange, though, lay at the other end of the country. Bartali asked Goddet to place it where he thought best. There wasn't anywhere obvious. Nobody had thought to build a statue in the *Parc des Princes* and it was ignominious to abandon a bouquet at the trackside. Goddet ordered a plaque to be put up in the offices of *L'Équipe* and Bartali's bouquet was placed beneath it.

3
The War Of The Gods

The year Bartali first won the Tour was 1938, his second attempt. Bartali won by 18 minutes, 27 seconds over the runner-up, Félicien Vervaecke, and 29 minutes, 26 seconds over the third man, Victor Cossan. He had trouble sleeping after each stage for fans shouting for him in the street. Georges Briquet, the voice of French radio from 1930 to the 1950s, wrote: "These people had found a superman. Outside Bartali's hotel at Aix-les-Bains an Italian general was holding back the crowd by shouting: 'Don't touch him—he's a god!'"

A pretty grumpy god, though, and far from saintly. He was boastful and miserable. Pierre Chany said the best that could be said of him is that he never contradicted his own stories. And since those stories usually concerned unwitnessed events high in the mountains, they couldn't be checked. In 1950 Bartali brushed shoulders or touched wheels—which isn't clear, like much of the story—in the Pyrenees. Bartali fell and Italian fans turned on Jean Robic, whom they took for the guilty man, punching him and waving a knife. And maybe French fans then went to his defense.

Bartali won the stage but an hour later said he wasn't going to ride where fans waved knives. He was going home. If that was odd then what followed was cruel. Bartali insisted all his team must go as well and that the second Italian team, with which he had no formal connection, must go too. Telling his own riders was bad. In those days many professionals made their money from village races, events on round-the-houses courses for which they were contracted because they had finished the Tour. They rode for Bartali in the Tour because teams shared what they won and the winner gave everything to his domestiques. Now Bartali's pride was depriving them of a living.

But telling the Cadetti they too must go was cruel. These second-string riders were on top of the world. Against all hopes, one of them—Fiorenzo Magni—was race leader. But Bartali was the most powerful man in Italian cycling. You crossed him at your peril. The Italians went home.

Bartali never changed his tale of the knifeman. Journalists were on the story straight away, of course. The most anyone could remember was a spectator who'd been slicing sausages for a sandwich when Robic fell in front of him. He got up from his chair to help, the knife and quite possibly the sausage still in his hands. Bartali had his reasons but nobody ever found out what.

Bartali was never warm. He liked recognition but his favorite expression was gloomy: "Everything's wrong; we'll have to start again." The sad thing is that both he and his younger rival ended their lives unhappily. Bartali lost his money, his waistline and eventually his mind. Jose-Miguel Echavarri used to warn the later Tour winner, Miguel Indurain: "Whatever you do, in later life don't become like Gino Bartali."

Fausto Coppi was the younger man. He died, broken in spirit, "a magnificent and grotesque washout", in Chany's words. His career was greater even than Bartali's, winning not only three Tours but also the world championship, the world hour record, the Giro d'Italia and more classics than any man might wish. When Coppi escaped, Raphaël Géminiani said, the judges didn't need stopwatches to measure his lead. The chimes of the village church would do just as well. "Paris–Roubaix? Milan–San Remo? Tour of Lombardy? We're talking ten minutes to a quarter of an hour. That's how Fausto Coppi was."

Coppi won the 1952 Tour by not much less than half an hour and Goddet had to double other prizes to keep the rest interested. From 1946 to 1954, according to Chany, Coppi was never caught once he had broken away.

The only thing that he and Bartali had in common was what several observers described as "a permanent air of sadness, cynicism almost, that only close friends could break." Whereas Bartali used his well-publicized religious belief and his connections with Pope Pius XII to avoid going to war, Coppi was captured by the British in the North African desert. Where Bartali ate with a crucifix on his table and visited shrines during races, Coppi was more neutral.

He never said he was an atheist but never denied it either. Which in an Italy both highly traditional and highly Roman Catholic was a striking position. The writer Curzio Malparte—his real name was Kurt Suckert; he chose Malparte, "bad start", as a play on Napoleon Bonaparte—summed it up this way: "Bartali belongs to those who believe in tradition. He is a metaphysical man protected by the saints. Coppi has nobody in heaven to take care of him. His manager, his masseur, have no wings. He is alone, alone on a bicycle. Bartali prays when he is pedaling; the rational Cartesian and skeptical Coppi is filled with doubts, believes only in his body."

Two things were extraordinary about Coppi: the first is that he was a cyclist and the second is that he was just a cyclist. His record as "a cyclist" speaks for itself. A director of *La Gazzetta dello Sport* wrote after his death: "I pray that the good God will one day soon send us another Coppi."

His record as "just a cyclist" is even more extraordinary because his private life not only split the nation and involved the police, but also brought the condemnation of God's spokesman on earth. Because he left his wife for a girlfriend. Coppi sweated and grimaced and got covered in grime. He didn't play in clothes just as suited to martinis in the bar. Nobody expected he was a saint. But there was outrage when he wasn't.

Coppi had a wife, Bruna. But he was pursued by what we'd now call a groupie, although a high-class one. Giulia Locatelli was, said Jean-Paul Ollivier in his biography of Coppi, "strikingly beautiful with thick chestnut hair divided into enormous plaits." She was pictured at Coppi's side, unidentified but wearing a white raincoat. Picture desks went through earlier shots and found she was there too. She was Coppi's lover: "the woman in white."

Coppi left his wife and Giulia moved in. Police raided them at midnight to check they weren't sharing a bed. Pope Pius XII refused to bless the Giro while Coppi was in it and sent a note saying Coppi's adultery had "caused him great pain." That a Pope who refused to condemn the slaughter of Jews in the second world war should worry whether a cyclist was having it away with his girlfriend is breathtaking. But it shows the position a man can have in life and in the affairs of a church with a billion adherents just because he does well in bicycle races.

On April 15, 1966, the magazine *Time* coined the name "Swinging London." It confirmed the decade as hip, carefree and the antithesis of the Fifties, dominated by the generation which took the world to war. It was a "bewitching" era, wrote the journalist Christopher Booker, even if in retrospect it was "odd and shallow and egocentric and even rather horrible." But it was also hip. Hip enough for Mick Jagger, miniskirts, the Pill, the British Invasion and Twiggy. Too hip, surely, to repeat the Bartali-Coppi story?

Well, no. The parallels are almost identical. For Bartali, the solid peasant who stood for traditional values, the smell of the earth and the honesty of small-scale farming, there was Raymond Poulidor. "He reassured people who found themselves overtaken by progress," said Jean-Luc Boeuf and Yves Léonard. For the new France of industrialization, modernization and the Space Age, there was Jacques Anquetil. "People who recognized themselves in Anquetil liked his emphasis on style and the elegance of the way he raced," said Boeuf and Léonard. "Behind this fluidity and appearance of ease was the image of a France that succeeded and it was people who took risks who identified with him."

The two men had only two years between them but Poulidor could have been a generation earlier. He spoke slowly, as people from Limoges do, and he spoke with the accent of the rural south. His face was lined and he grimaced with effort. He spent his first prizes on cows for the family farm. He had never traveled in a train until the army called him for compulsory service. By then Anquetil, high-cheeked, smooth-faced, blond hair swept upwards, had traveled to Finland and won an Olympic medal.

The links between Coppi and Anquetil, both supposedly city slickers although neither was, would have been all the stronger had the world known about Anquetil's sexual shenanigans. He too made off with a married woman. But he went further. While still married to Janine, he had an affair with her daughter by her first marriage, which led to a further daughter. He then had an affair with the wife of Janine's son.

Poulidor, on the other hand, is still married to Gisèle and still lives in St-Léonard-de-Noblat, near where he was born. He doesn't hold the record for second places in the Tour but he's remembered for it because he could never outflank Anquetil. Except in time-trials, Poulidor was the better. He was stronger on the flat and he was the better climber. But Anquetil repeatedly outwitted him. Anquetil won without making an effort he didn't have to make, and became rich and lived in a château; Poulidor worked hard, made a fight of it, always came second. Like Vietto, he was the self-image of men who believed they toiled while others profited. And because that mental divide couldn't be closed, it split France.

Pierre Chany wrote, perhaps without expecting to be believed: "The Tour de France has the major fault of dividing the country, right down to the smallest hamlet, even families, into two rival camps. I know a man who grabbed his wife and held her on the grill of a heated stove, seated and with her skirt held up, for favoring Jacques Anquetil when he preferred Raymond Poulidor. The following year, the woman became a Poulidor-iste. But it was too late. The husband had switched his allegiance to Gimondi. The last I heard, they were digging their heels in and the neighbors were complaining."

Poulidor hasn't raced for decades. He makes a living from being Raymond Poulidor, a living he concedes would be nowhere near as good had he ever worn the *maillot jaune*. He is as much amused as distressed that his name has become a synonym for someone destined to fail, someone unlucky or even someone who doesn't try hard enough and gets the consequences. Anquetil, on the other hand—not least for what now looks misguided honesty in saying he took drugs and he could see no reason not to—is dead and a faint national embarrassment.

4

The I Of The Needle

One Saturday night, Louison Bobet was at a dinner for winners of the Tour de France, hosted by Jacques Goddet and Félix Lévitan. They were in illustrious company for in the room were Nicolas Frantz, who won in 1927 and '28, through to Eddy Merckx, the last of whose five wins was in 1974. In all there were eleven winners from seven countries, twenty-seven victories among them. Among the journalists was Jean Leulliot.

"The riders were like kids," he reported, "going round collecting each other's autographs. One table deserved particular attention: the one that grouped Anquetil, Merckx and Bobet, thirteen wins in the Tour between them. The conversation was particularly lively and Louison Bobet was being challenged for daring to say he had never taken the slightest stimulant or tonic. He was obliged to say that he had swallowed small bottles prepared by his soigneur of the era without knowing exactly what they contained. Which made Jacques Anquetil and Eddy Merckx laugh."

Bobet was fussy about hygiene when most riders wore their single jersey for a week without washing it, when they scrubbed two to a tub in water others had used before them. In 1947 he refused to wear the yellow jersey because, thanks to a sponsor which made artificial fabric, it wasn't pure wool. Another had to be found overnight.

He was right to be anxious because he was troubled by saddle sores. The Tour until the 1960s had no doctor. In the 1940s the job, such as it existed, was done by Henri Manchon, "directeur sportif and general soigneur," whose qualifications were hanging around riders at the *Vélodrome d'Hiver*, of which he was general manager. He went from hotel to hotel, helping where he could, dishing out treatment. And in 1948, he made what appears now an extraordinary statement but which then barely raised comment.

Bobet, who was in a position to win the Tour but finally finished fourth, came close to dropping out because once more a boil was causing agony. Manchon told waiting reporters that doctors had lanced it and given him 200 milligrams of penicillin. Things looked to be improving. When reporters asked what caused the problem, he replied "exhaustion, eating too much and perhaps also misusing strengtheners."

The splendidly-named George Pilkington Mills of the Anfield Bicycle Club said he rode the 1891 Bordeaux–Paris a whole day faster than expected thanks to eating strawberries. Nobody knows. Contemporary reports, though, talk of "speed cracks" shouting for "acid" to be handed to them.

By the time the British returned to Bordeaux–Paris in 1896, their winner—Arthur Linton—was openly professional. And openly drugged. To get through the 500 or so kilometers, he hired a controversial manager called Choppy Warburton, a man the American writer Dick Swann called "a sharp dresser and flamboyant personality, given to extra-long topcoats with many pockets, and gaudy waistcoats. In England, the home of the Gentleman Amateur, he was heartily disliked, feared and in fact hated by the National Cyclists Union."

Nobody knows what Linton gave riders. A surprising number died young, although "weakened by doping" was never on their death certificates. The reporter from *Cyclers' News* wrote: "I saw [Linton] at Tours, half way through the race, at midnight, where he came in with glassy eyes and tottering limbs, and in a high state of nervous excitement. At Orléans, at five o'clock in the morning, Choppy and I looked after a wreck—a corpse as Choppy called him."

And yet Linton won, sharing victory with Gaston Rivière after each blamelessly took different routes to the finish. Nine weeks later he was dead, of typhoid fever. People who say shenanigans started in cycling with the police swoop on the Tour de France in 1998 are more than a century out. Or, if you're talking of sport in general, longer.

Jean-Pierre de Mondenard is a gentle, balding bespectacled man with a face saddened by life. He is the world authority on the history of doping, author of 40 books on sports medicine, and doctor at the Tour de France from 1973 to 1975. He traces doping, in intent if not medical knowledge, to prehistory. Drug-taking as it interests us, though, he traces to long-distance walking races in Britain in the nineteenth century, citing the confession of Abraham Wood in 1807 that he had dosed himself with laudanum, a tincture of opium. From there the habit spread to six-day cycle races.

Road riders were more interested in dulling the long, cold hours on rough roads and heavy bikes. Drugs weren't to go faster, although all the better if that's what they did. They were to make life tolerable. Races stunk of ether, which riders breathed from scarves or handkerchiefs under their chin. When they weren't numb from that, they were half-cut on wine. Clean drinking water wasn't widespread in nineteenth century France. By the time towns had it by the start of the twentieth, the world war wrecked purification plants and distribution pipes and polluted the land with corpses human and animal.

From there grew the belief, not unfounded, that water from a faucet wasn't trustworthy. Wine and beer, on the other hand, had been treated commercially. Solution: drink beer and wine. Consequence: alarming alcoholism. Right into the 1950s, riders taking drinks from spectators were treated to cider in Normandy, wine in the south, beer in the northeast. Water wasn't always an option.

And then there was hocus-pocus. De Mondenard says: "Certain products were prepared and sold specifically for cyclists. In 1892, a drink with the evocative name of Vélo-Guignolet [guignolet is an alcoholic drink with cherries] was all the fashion. Made to a recipe attributed to Jeanne de la Noue, founder in 1704 of the Order of Sisters de la Providence de Nôtre-Dame des Ardilliers, it was, according to the firm's advertising, 'the best of drinks, the best tonic, the most efficient.' Its precious qualities meant it was adopted by the *vélocemen* of France.

"In 1894, Dr Léon Petit offered medical advice in the weekly publication, *La Bicyclette*. Replying to a question about what to take to make long-distance riding easier, he replied: 'Go to see Monsieur Grenet, pharmacist at 20 rue des Sablons in Paris, and ask him to make you some of the stimulant potion that he provided for Louis Cottereau during the last Bordeaux–Paris. Take a glass of it every four hours of the race.'"

Nobody cared about doping in the Tour. The era and its mores were different and cycling was a lower-class sport disputed by and watched by men who knew what it was to ache in fields or mines. If *coureurs* took something to make life bearable, good for them. It was no more than peasants with red wine.

In 1952, the year after "general soigneur" Henri Manchon died, the Tour looked for a real doctor and found a short, stocky judoka who had studied at the national medical school. Pierre Dumas was a strange and a good choice. He had little interest in cycling and no more knowledge than he gained from newspapers. He was more interested in judo and climbing. But that was also his strength. Manchon had been too close and his role in the organization meant conflict of interest. Added to which he wasn't a doctor.

Dumas, too, went from hotel to hotel. And he was horrified. In a paper to the Council of Europe in 1964, he told of "soigneurs, *fakirs* who came from the six-days. Their value was in what they had in their cases. Riders took anything they were given, even bee stings and toad extract. [There was] medicine from the heart of Africa, healers laying on hands or giving out irradiating balms, feet plunged into unbelievable mixtures which could lead to eczema, so-called magnetized diets and everything else you could imagine."

After that, he said, they began reading Vidal, the drugs directory. A French coach told him how a rider would "at the finish of a race run wild in a manner that his defeat does not entirely justify" and of riders who didn't realize until hours after their victory that they had won. "I have also seen slobbering cyclists on the roadside," the coach told Dumas, "their mouths foaming. They are ill-tempered and kick their bikes to smash them, making disordered gesticulations. Another hits his head with a bottle of mineral water he has just been given. Yet another throws himself at the barrier and breaks it. This would be comical if it were not so important and pitiable."

Marcel Bidot, manager of the French team in 1960, said: "Three-quarters of the riders are doped. I am well placed to know since I visit their rooms each evening. I always leave frightened."

British troops took 72 million doses of amphetamine in the war. Pilots took it too but so many crashed that in 1943 the Royal Air Force withdrew it. After the war the untainted reputation kept production going. Unused military supplies were sold or stolen. Amphetamine was part of slimming tablets. Eight thousand million tablets were produced in the United States in 1966, enough to give every man, woman and child 35 doses of 5 milligrams every year. Being, incidentally, about the quantity that cyclists took for everyday races. Although some took more...

In 1954, Leandro Faggin was about to win the amateur pursuit championship. Karel Steyaert wrote: "His feverish eyes were deep into his face and he kept licking his dry lips as though he had a thirst but nothing to help it. They were signs that no doctor would mistake, and we all knew he had taken something. I pointed him out to several colleagues and in no time there was a crowd of soigneurs, journalists and managers. Someone shouted: 'Nobody smoke in case there's an explosion!'"

The Dutch reporter and broadcaster, Theo Komen, wrote in *25 Jaar Doping* of round-the-houses races. The tradition was that riders asked to change in a garage or inside room. He spoke of a race in which riders changed at a bakery. The baker, enjoying the celebrity, stood, chatted and watched. And he saw every rider inject himself. It was, each said, "for diabetes."

The first international scare came in 1955, when the Tour rode from Marseille to Avignon by way of Mont Ventoux. A French rider, a man with dark, wavy hair, Jean Malléjac, was "streaming with sweat, haggard and comatose, zigzagging, and the road wasn't wide enough for him," wrote the Tour archivist, Jacques Augendre. "He was no longer in the real world, still less in the world of cyclists and the Tour de France."

An official of another team, Sauveur Ducazeaux—a restaurateur in Paris for his day job—pulled him off the road. Malléjac collapsed "completely unconscious," said Pierre Chany, "his face the color of a corpse, a freezing sweat on his forehead." Dumas arrived and, according to the *Télégramme de Brest*, "he had to force his jaws apart to make him drink and it was a quarter of an hour later, after he had had an injection of solucamphor and been given oxygen, that Malléjac regained consciousness. Taken by ambulance, he hadn't however completely recovered. He fought, he gesticulated, demanded his bike, wanted to get out."

The French author, Antoine Blondin, wrote of riders so crazed on Mont Ventoux that they rode down instead of up and brandished their pumps at spectators. They were, he said, "reduced to madness under the effect of heat or stimulants."

Malléjac gave a guarded television interview in which he was asked: "Was there ever a time when a soigneur passed you a bottle that could have contained dope?"

"Perhaps, yes. It's possible. Without accusing anyone, but…(pause) it's difficult to say but there were times when I would have liked to have analyzed what was in certain bottles. I'd had stomach troubles for two days and I was suffering a bit as soon as we left Marseille. I was in a good position at the bottom of Mont Ventoux. We started on the col and I began to weaken. I remember a spectator poured water on my back and my cap and I fell a short distance beyond him. I don't remember any more because I was unconscious for quarter of an hour. It's like when you faint, you can't say what happened. So far as I was concerned, I had fainted."

"The morning of that stage, did the soigneur give you a bottle?"

"Yes. "

"Did you drink from it before you collapsed?"

"Yes, half an hour, three-quarters of an hour before."

"Did you notice an unusual flavor?"

Malléjac starts to smile, then says: "Not particularly. It was just a bit bitter, like a cola."

"Was the bottle found after the accident?"

"Yes, it was still in my pocket. I remember, in the ambulance, that it was still in my pocket. They took it out of my jersey and removed my jersey and put it all in the netting above my head."

"Was there an analysis of what it held?"

"I asked them to. But they said that when they found the bottle it was empty. But I'm certain that it wasn't empty. It's curious."

"That suggests it contained dope."

"I can't confirm it. It's possible. I don't want to accuse anyone but I would like to know what that bottle held so I can take action against the person who gave it to me."

He was never able to. Dumas said he would start a claim against persons unknown for attempted murder. But there the matter rested. The interview was broadcast on July 11, 1967. Two days later it had been surpassed: Tom Simpson dropped dead on the same climb.

5
Everyone Takes Something

Jacques Anquetil has decomposed over the years into a two-wheel pharmacy box. It is the price of his honesty. "It's not possible for a man, however gifted he is as an athlete, to race almost every day without using stimulants," he said in a television debate with François Missoffe, the sports minister, in 1967. "You'd have to be naive or a hypocrite to insist that the Tour de France, Bordeaux–Paris, a Dauphiné Libéré, can be ridden on just mineral water…All the riders take something."

But, Théo Komen pointed out, stars took less than ordinary riders. They had class, using amphetamine to top it up. Mundane riders, domestiques who exhausted their bodies in service of stars but still had to survive a race in which they were outclassed, had to impress as well. Their living depended on it. The stars took enough to get through the day, then a sleeping pill to overcome the effects. They slept; the also-rans, in the words of a Dutch rider, "joined the League of Ceiling-Starers."

The need to impress was enormous. This, remember, was when many so-called professionals were paid nothing but their board and keep and a share of prizes. Riding *à la musette*. The rather gross Dutch manager, Kees Pellenaars, all pudgy face, belly and cigar, told of that eagerness in his biography, *Daar Was't,* in 1973. He took a promising prospect to a training camp in Spain.

"The boy changed then into a sort of lion. He raced around as though he was powered by rockets. I went to talk to him. He was really happy that he was riding so well and he told me to look out for him. I asked him if perhaps he wasn't 'using something', and he jumped straight up, climbed on a chair and from deep inside a closet pulled out a plastic bag full of pills. I felt my heart skip a beat. I had never seen so many fireworks together.

"With a soigneur and another rider, we counted the pills: there were five thousand of them, excluding hormone preparations and sleeping pills. I took the five thousand bombs away, to his own relief. I let him keep the hormones and the sleeping pills. Later he seemed to have taken too many at once and he slept for a couple of days on end. We couldn't wake him up. We took him to hospital and they pumped out his stomach. They tied him to his bed to prevent anything going wrong again. But somehow he had some stimulant and fancied taking a walk. A nurse came across him in the corridor, walking along with the bed strapped to his back."

Anquetil never argued for excesses like that. His insistence was that a professional was doing a job. Rudi Altig summed it up after refusing a test at the 1966 world championship: "We are not sportsmen; we are earning our living." Or as Geoffrey Nicholson of the London *Guardian* put the argument: "As swotting students and long-distance truck drivers took Benzedrine to keep them awake, and practically everyone else took a coffee break when he was flagging, so cyclists were entitled to take some sort of artificial aid to help them through the extreme rigors of their trade."

Chany said: "Jacques had the strength—for which he was always criticized—to say out loud what others would only whisper. So, when I asked him, 'What have you taken?' he didn't drop his eyes before replying. He had the strength of conviction."

On July 13, 1967, Tom Simpson died on Mt. Ventoux with empty pill bottles in his pockets.

Drug tests had started in the Tour the previous year. One of the few not to flee was Raymond Poulidor. He was walking through his hotel in Bordeaux when testers, not recognizing one of the best-known faces in the country, asked if he was riding the Tour. Poulidor said he was and became the first rider in Tour history to be tested.

Next day riders pedaled five kilometres out of the city, to La House near Canéjan, and began walking. With as much elegance as the slogan demanded, they yelled: "*Pissez! Pissez! Pissez!*" Nicholson said: "The implication was clear: any more testing, no more Tour. The samples taken from Poulidor's bedroom were never mentioned again." Goddet's demand that the commissaires find the ringleaders came to nothing, although the local historian, Hervé Mathurin, said: "It certainly seems Jacques Anquetil wasn't the least involved; he was considered a suspect because he had refused a test in Liège–Bastogne–Liège some months earlier."

Simpson never denied taking drugs. He had a heavy reputation in the bunch, said Maurice Vidal of *Miroir Sprint*. Simpson said he had a wife and daughters to support; he'd stop taking drugs when others stopped. They doubtless said they'd stop when he stopped. *Paris-Match* spoke of his taste for money and gain, a reluctance to pay tax and his escape from Britain to avoid draft into the army. He took part in the strike, angry, as Poulidor said in *La Gloire sans Maillot Jaune*, that "we were treated as though we were all druggies. No profession would accept that." But he walked hidden in the crowd, not happy to draw attention to a problem he felt best hidden.

Simpson lost much of a season after he broke his leg when skiing. He needed to ride well in the Tour, possibly winning a stage, to keep in a team, to keep being paid. He told *L'Équipe*: "The Tour de France is the most celebrated and the most reported of bike races, and so that's where you have to get yourself noticed by managers." The implied missing words, said Charroin Pascal in the *International Review on Sport and Violence*, were "at any price."

Close to the top of the Ventoux, where a memorial now stands, he zigzagged, fell, set off again, then fell unconscious. Three men ran to his rescue, all in shorts, two without shirts. The heat was enough to melt the road. A gendarme drove down the mountain to find Pierre Dumas. There had been a *pépin*, he said, a spot of bother. Dumas accelerated past a straggle of riders accompanied by his assistant, a man called Macorig. The three barelegged men, now part of a small crowd, had started mouth-to-mouth resuscitation. Among them was one of the team's mechanics, Harry Hall. Another mechanic, Ken Bird, drove into the countryside that evening and buried a white Tupperware box holding Simpson's drugs, for fear the police would find it first. "Unless the road has been changed or the place has been built over, I could take you to the precise spot and find it," he said.

Dumas said Simpson died where he fell, his death confirmed after his body arrived at St-Marthe hospital in Avignon by helicopter. In his jersey pockets were three small tubes. Two were empty. The third contained a mixture of Stenamina and Tonédron, amphetamines. Burial permission was refused.

The Tour was embarrassed. France, too, said J. L. Manning of the London *Daily Mail*. A man who once thought it "a jolly thought" that athletes were to wee into bottles wrote: "Is France trying to hush up the scandals of the Tour? I say yes. The first act of hushing up is not to attempt detection, let alone waiting a year before taking action. How much husher can you get?

"Three days after this year's race [1967], the French authorities announced that next October and November, a French and Italian rider would be prosecuted for alleged doping offenses in last year's Tour [1966]. France had surrendered the need rigorously to prevent doping to the discreet requirement of not tackling it on a big tourist occasion until a year had passed safely. That is my accusation: I nail it firmly to the wall."

Simpson's death forced cycling's hand. His team manager, Alec Taylor, said it was terrified. "Before Tom's death I saw on the Continent the overcautious way riders were tested for dope, as if the authorities feared to lift the veil, scared of how to handle the results, knowing all the while what they would be."

Prominent voices insisted drugs hadn't killed Simpson. The inquest blamed heatstroke and heart failure, only noting the presence of drugs. Anquetil and his team manager, Raphaël Géminiani, said Simpson could have been saved by an injection of Maxiton to restart his heart, but Maxiton, said Géminiani, was impossible because cycling's rules made it impossible. It brought an educated sneer from de Mondenard: "Raphaël Géminiani, a rider at a high level, specialist in revitalization ('All the riders of my generation took drugs'), allows himself thanks to 'medical knowledge' acquired from the saddle of a bicycle to pass judgment on the competence of a doctor."

Simpson fans still deny he died of drugs. He had a heart attack. "The drugs didn't kill Tom," said Harry Hall, the mechanic who tried to save him. "Tom killed himself." To them and specifically to Géminiani, Philippe Miserez, chief doctor on the Tour from 1972 to 1981, said in *L'Équipe* on July 22, 1988: "I like Gem but what he says is ridiculous. It's all false, utterly false, and the worst thing is that he knows it himself, I'm certain. He has astonishing selective amnesia. When he says Tom Simpson died from a heart attack, it's obviously true, but the attack was made irreversible by doping products. If there was a killer in the affair, it was the manager of the British team who should have stopped his rider before it was too late." Taylor, the manager, said he hadn't realized Simpson was anything but groggy. He thought the cold air of the descent would revive him and worried only that he would take risks to make up time.

Dope tests followed in profusion but the equipment was primitive. De Mondenard said it found only a few drugs and only "in equine quantities." Tests couldn't distinguish between amphetamines and traces of medicines and cold cures. Riders became proficient at tricking controls with bottles of other people's urine, the control supervisors seemingly not surprised that samples were cold. The legend grew that a Dutch rider—a man—had been found innocent of drugs but guilty of being pregnant.

The origins are in a story that Anquetil wrote in *France Dimanche* when he didn't ride the Tour in which Simpson died. He went into the tricks and hidden scandals of cycling, telling all. French cycling, far from pleased at being alerted so it could do something about it, turned on Anquetil instead and banned him from riding the national and the world championships.

"After a race in his home town," Anquetil wrote, "the Dutchman Piet Rentmeester was asked to urinate in a flask.

"'I can't,' he replied.

"'Well,' an official told him, 'we can't hang about here. Go back to your house, fill up the bottle as soon as you can and bring it back to us.' Three hours later, Rentmeester brought back the filled bottle. Two weeks later, after the analysis, he was told that there was no trace of dope. But on the other hand, whoever had urinated in the bottle was undeniably…pregnant. For the good reason that it was Mrs Rentmeester."

Rentmeester and his wife became accepted truth. But decades later it dawned on Leon Schattenberg, the Dutch federation doctor, that dope tests weren't pregnancy tests. Not then. Now they would show up pregnancy because they look for hormones. But then testers looked for amphetamine and not much else. Schattenberg went to Rentmeester's house in Yerseke, a waterside town in Zeeland, and asked him: Had it ever happened? And no it hadn't. But it made Anquetil's point that drug tests were haphazard and easily cheated.

Jacques Goddet reflected in 1999: "I feel real resentment towards the medical and scientific powers who have deceived us for 30 years.

There were 107 controls in the 1998 Tour"—in 1998 the police arrested riders and team officials, and a trial established that there was system-atic doping in the Tour—"and they were all negative. The controls are almost always negative, which means that the labs have been making serious mistakes, mistakes that have only served to speed up the growth of this evil. The controls that we developed after Simpson's death were a lie, covered up by the highest scientific and medical authorities."

He didn't go into detail.

6

My Sponsor Right Or Wrong

Tom Simpson died not in the colors of his Peugeot team but in another white jersey: the makeshift outfit, with a Union Jack on each shoulder, of a British team sponsored for the occasion by an importer of bananas. To explain it needs a change of historical gears.

For decades, sponsors were drawn from companies that made bicycles and supplied tires. No other sponsors were allowed. There were cars on the road but only for the rich. The cycling community, said *The Cyclist,* was "the great clerk class and the great shop assistant class." Everyone but the rich walked, was pulled by a horse or pedaled a bike. Bicycles established social status as cars often do now. Since one bicycle is much like another, factories competed on image. Their machines floated effortlessly. "Cycling is like flying," boasted Pope Manufacturing in Hartford, Connecticut. "You have longed for the wings of a bird! They are yours in the Columbia. Light, strong, swift, beautiful—a Columbia will carry you where your will directs—and bring you home safe again."

A character reflects in *Three Men on the Bummel*: "On only one poster that I can recollect have I seen the rider represented as doing any work. But this man was being pursued by a bull. In ordinary cases the object of the artist is to convince the hesitating neophyte that the sport of bicycling consists in sitting on a luxurious saddle, and being moved rapidly in the direction you wish to go by unseen heavenly powers. Generally speaking, the rider is a lady, and then one feels that for perfect bodily rest combined with entire freedom from mental anxiety, slumber upon a water-bed cannot compare with bicycle-riding upon a hilly road."

For those who couldn't be convinced that cycling was effortless, there was the contradictory tactic of showing how hard it was:

employing men to ride improbable distances faster than a horse. Teams competed between themselves and with the sport generally. In 1930 Henri Desgrange despaired and dismissed them from the Tour, inviting riders to compete for their country instead. To pay the cost, he allowed an advertising procession to lead the race. The advertisers came from outside the cycle industry and saw the publicity value in an era without television advertising.

Until 1950, bike sales held up. Benjo Maso writes in *Wij Waren Allemaal Goden*: "While Coppi and Bartali were fighting out their immortal duels in the Tour, the French were buying 1,300,000 bikes, or 300,000 more than the previous best year of 1938. But then sales fell, from 1950 onwards. In 1951 they dropped to less than a million for the first time, a year later to 750,000, and in 1957 came a new low of 534,000.

"The recession had nothing to do with the riders that followed Coppi, nor with the popularity of the Tour de France. It came from the arrival of the moped. In 1948 France had made only 40,000; by 1956 that figure had risen above 900,000. Most bike factories had neither the capital nor the expertise to compete in this new market. Many slid into serious problems. Several had to close. And just as at the start of the 1930s, few firms would or could pay for a bike team."

The first *extra-sportif*—a sponsor from outside the bike trade—was a soccer betting company called ITP, in Britain in 1947. There were others in Spain but Spain was too far from big-time cycling, and the promoters of road racing in Britain, the British League of Racing Cyclists, were outside UCI rules.

Then in 1954 a balding Italian called Fiorenzo Magni negotiated a deal with Nivea. Riders used Nivea to reduce friction in their shorts but the German company that made it intended it as face cream—an episode of great hilarity because Magni was ugly. He recalled: "They gave me 20 million lire [about €200,000 or $260,000]. This was for everything the team needed. At the end of the year there wasn't much left. But they were very generous and gave me a check for a similar amount plus they renewed our agreement for two more years. If you remember that cycling was more popular than soccer and that I was the first to do this then you can understand the success of this action. Nivea always thanked me for my idea, even years later. This was the beginning of the salvation of cycling."

Traditional sponsors saw themselves being edged out by business-men who knew nothing of cycling and wanted to exploit it without sentiment. Nor was *L'Équipe* happy. Ordinary papers, like *Le Parisien Libéré* (now simply *Le Parisien*), have a constant sale, some days better than others but every week much the same. Sales of *L'Équipe*, though, trebled with a big event and slumped when it finished. Its biggest sales were during the Tour, which was when it made profits. They came from sales but much more from advertising. Allow that on riders' backs and the paper cut its throat.

L'Équipe organized Paris–Roubaix and ordered Magni to stay away unless he wore his national champion's jersey instead. By then even stars like Fausto Coppi were having trouble finding sponsors. And even if they found one in the cycle industry, those outside paid better. Coppi said he'd ride only if Magni was allowed his Nivea colors. Magni said: "The French didn't want to lose Coppi so I raced with my jersey that day and every other day!"

The row grew when Raphaël Géminiani approached Max Augier, director of the St-Raphaël aperitif company that shared his name. St Raphaël was the archangel the drink's inventor praised when he hit on the drink's formula, and thereby his own fortune, in 1830. Géminiani, on the other hand, was neither angel nor saint. The UCI told Gémin-iani the deal was illegal. Géminiani refused to budge. The stalemate lasted until Milan–San Remo, the first classic. But duplicity achieves much. Achille Joinard, the president of the UCI, said no with his lips but yes with his head.

Pierre Chany said: "Officially, the UCI was against extra-sportifs but Joinard, a clear-thinking man, had come to see they were an inevi-table evolution. So, he winked as he warned Raphaël, convinced that history would soon prove him right. But more, and this is just a per-sonal opinion, I think it didn't distress him to poke a stick into Jacques Goddet's wheels. Whatever, Milan–San Remo started at eight o'clock and the official telegram didn't arrive until ten o'clock, when Gémin-iani and his band were already riding in St-Raphaël jerseys."

The gates opened. Helyett, another French bicycle company, joined Leroux, a chicory maker. Money from Leroux's instant cof-fee let Helyett take on a young Jacques Anquetil. Émile Mercier went higher and interested British Petroleum. And so it went on: Pelforth beer, Grammont television sets, Solo margarine, more international names such as Ford, Esso and EMI, all on the backs of pedaling sandwich men.

Companies used to international business were less tolerant than bike companies. Cycle manufacturers could advertise riders' successes even in national colors. The brash new sponsors weren't happy to get no more than a stenciled cloth pinned to their riders' jerseys in the year's biggest race. And in 1961 they combined with the few bike companies left as primary sponsors to force their way back into the Tour.

Goddet struggled to smile. "The structure of professional cycling is unhappily in a weak state," he wrote. "And while I like national teams for their dignity and their symbolic value, it's obvious that this formula would have to be expanded to have any significance. At the moment only five countries can put up a worthwhile team. Trade teams, it seems to me, are therefore the most natural and balanced."

Trade teams didn't end the problems. They worsened them. The new sponsors were more powerful than bike factories. They had a grip on the sport and they had a grip on the advertising they took, or didn't take, in *L'Équipe*. Félix Lévitan was sure they were behind the strike at Bordeaux in 1966. He never explained how but that didn't matter: Lévitan wasn't shy of telling journalists their role was to venerate the Tour, and the idea that sponsors could humiliate the race and therefore him was intolerable. They were sent out of class. In 1967 the Tour would be "remoralized", returned to national teams. It was a boon for some—the British could enter and Simpson, the only conceivable leader, was free of competition within the Peugeot team—but it wasn't a success.

Goddet used to care for the sporting side of the Tour while Lévitan scraped in the money. His technique was lots of small sponsorships, for best climber, for the friendliest rider, a third for computers and clocks, another for the ambulance, direction signs, motorbikes, anything. There could be sixty of them. It was a mess which only the eventual appointment of Jean-Marie Leblanc put right. But while it lasted, Lévitan was proud of his system and sensitive, as always, to criticism. And criticism there had been.

Using the sponsors' supposed troublemaking as justification, he set about keeping the Tour as commercial as ever but making it seem less so—a riddle that Tour organizers have set themselves since 1903.

Geoffrey Nicholson explained: "What the Tour did to placate the opposition in 1967 was to play the patriotic card. It scrapped trade teams in favor of national teams, since a contest between squads in French and Belgian colors would appear less blatantly commercial than one between Ford-France-Gitane and Flandria-Romeo. It was being done, said *L'Équipe*, the voice of the Tour, 'in response to the noble and superior interests of the race, to the wishes of the public and the desires of the public authorities.'

"The sponsors had to accept the change, but did so with ill-grace. The new arrangement, they argued, was basically unfair: they paid their riders' salaries all summer only to be denied publicity from the season's major event. They also pointed to the danger of collusion between trade-team colleagues of different nationalities."

In other words, they complained of what they complained about in 1930, except that before 1930 they had been complaining about just the opposite—that instead of commercial colleagues forming combines, national combines were forming between rival colleagues. Nicholson says combines did occur in 1967, and that "loyalties were put under so much strain that the experiment was dropped after only two seasons. Since then nobody has seriously suggested reviving it except as an occasional variation."

But now, the Tour has become even more commercially angled. Cycling rules once demanded most of a team's riders came from the same country. Each team could have only a few foreigners, an arrangement which favored strong countries but proved disastrous for Simpson, who had no British trade team to ride for and who died in the attempt to impress a foreign one.

The rule demanded no more than one in five foreigners. Riders couldn't overturn it and spectators liked it because they could know a Peugeot rider was almost certainly French, or a Bianchi rider Italian. France and Italy saw no reason to change a system that gave their riders security. What makes the Simpson business doubly sad is that he probably never knew the rule had been illegal for ten years. The Treaty of Rome which set up the Common Market, now the European Union, ruled that a worker from one country had the right to work in another. No Belgian could be turned down in France because he was Belgian, no Spaniard turned away in Holland and no Briton kept out of a French team because he wasn't French.

Well, cycling news in 1957 wasn't the Treaty of Rome. It was France winning thirteen of the twenty-four stages in the Tour, and that Maurice Garin had breathed his last. The shock came from an improbable direction. Bruno Walrave was, and still is, a Dutchman who rides Derny pacing motorcycles in six-days and, back then, the huge pacing machines used in world championships. Riders employed him and he got on with the job. The UCI gave medals to both rider and pacer. It couldn't have two nations on the same rung of the podium so pacers and riders had to be from the same country. Walrave insisted at the Montreal championships in 1974 that he could sell his services to anyone. If the UCI stopped him, it was denying his right to have an employer from another European Union country.

He and another Dutch pacer, Nobby Koch, went to the European Court. Europe's judges didn't find it difficult. They ruled that the rules applied as much to cycling riders and officials as builders and truckers. Ever since, teams have employed riders from wherever they choose. Discovery Channel, an "American" team in 2007, had a Belgian manager and riders from fifteen countries. There were six Americans but most of the team was European and two were Asian. Even Discovery Channel itself was set up with foreign help, some of the funding coming from the BBC in Britain. Cycling was no longer a French sport in which others were invited to join.

Part five: Flamme Rouge

One of the first conventions in the Tour was to wave a red triangular flag to show the final kilometre. It was later hung above the road, these days from an inflatable arch. It's known in French as the "flamme rouge", the red flame.

1

The Eagle Has Landed

Cycling in the USA died. Or lay panting at best. America was unique in coming out of the second world war more prosperous than it entered. Roosevelt stemmed the Depression but the war reversed it. There were still poor people but many more who weren't poor, and unrivaled numbers achieved the dream of a job, a house and a car in the Eisenhower suburbs. But cycling lost out. Bikes in the 1950s were cumbersome, fat-tired balloon bombers, mock motorcycles or even aeroplanes, sold as toys. America had become a one-, two- even three-car society.

In 1919 Eisenhower joined an army expedition across America with 42 trucks, motorcycles, cars, ambulance, repair teams, field kitchens and searchlight teams. It left Washington on July 7 and in the first three days achieved a shade more than five and a half miles a day. Axles broke, tires bogged into nonexistent roads. It took until September 6 to get to San Francisco and it started Eisenhower "thinking about good two-lane highways," as he put it. By 1929 almost 80 percent of the world's cars were in America. There was one for every 5 people, compared to one for 33 in France and 6,130 in Russia. Until the 1920s fuel was sold in unlabelled cans. By 1929 there were 143,000 gas stations. Highways joined town to town, city to city and state to state. Never had cars been such a symbol of not just status but escape and discovery. Who'd want to do that on a bike?

And then came the Vietnam war and, even before it ended, the first of the 1970s oil crises. In 1973 Arab nations objected to what they saw as America's support for Israel in the Yom Kippur war and cut off exports. In 1979 a separate shortage struck after the fall of the Shah of Iran. For Jim McGurn, that was when cycling breathed again. He wrote: "Cycling became, for some Americans, a patriotic means of saving the nation's oil reserves. The great majority of machines bought at this time were heavy, multi-geared imitations of racing cycles. The American bicycle boom developed along recreational rather than utilitarian or specifically radical lines. It intensified in the late 1970s, boosted by the development of a strong popular interest in health and fitness."

Peter Nye said: "Health-conscious baby boomers were buying bicycles in unprecedented numbers. In 1971, 8.5 million bicycles were sold, more than double the 3.7 million sold in 1960. What distinguished the new sales was the shift in riders: one-third of the bicycles sold in 1971 were for adults. The new cyclists were not just riding their bikes: they were racing them. ABL membership tripled to 3,000 by 1968 and nearly tripled again by 1973 to 8,600."

Until then, a big event might attract 50. There were only 200 registered racers in the whole of California at the end of the 1950s. Most of their events were informal burn-ups or uncontrolled charges round a couple of blocks or the length of a street. A few legendary creatures had raced abroad and spoke with affected Italian accents. Into their midst fell a short, quiet young man called Mike Hiltner.

Hiltner is as unknown in the USA now as he was then. Part of that is that in 1978 he changed his name to Victor Vincente of America. He became a hippie, with long hair, a thick, long beard, sunken cheeks and a look of withdrawal from the world. He won the California road championship in 1958, which was creditable but not astounding given how limited was the competition. What was more remarkable was that the following year he went to the Tour du St-Laurent in Canada and, at eighteen, became its youngest winner. In 1960 he rode the team time-trial at the Rome Olympics—the race in which a Dane died from the heat, drugs and heart failure that killed Simpson—and came eleventh of thirty. Hiltner and others stayed in Italy, taking coffee dosed with amphetamine to ride races, then returned to California with a body "blown", as he put it, from the drugs he had taken.

George Mount was six at the time. While he too lives now in California, he was then still in his parents' house in New Jersey, from where he was eventually thrown out for refusing to join the army. In 1976 he came sixth in the Olympic road race in Montreal, the first American in the top 60 since 1912. It made him almost a god in a sport which, in the USA, had suffered an inferiority complex for as long as anyone remembered.

Mount and his teammate Mike Neel left to race in Europe. Neel was disillusioned after crashing in the rain in the Olympics, the race for which he had lived, and there was nothing left for him in American racing. He went to Italy and joined the cut-price Magniflex team, sponsored by a mattress factory. Mount said: "Neel started saying 'Hey, I know this kid in the States who could come over and kick all your guys' butts' and in the end the manager said 'Well, you better get him over.'" Mount was hanging on for the Olympics in Moscow. Then Jimmy Carter said there'd be no American team because of the Soviet Union's involvement in Afghanistan.

"As soon as I heard," Mount said, "I called Europe and I was lucky. This team made me an offer because the sponsor wanted to sell abroad and I was young and stupid and I said 'Hey, they're offering almost no money but I can live on it.'" And so he turned pro. And in 1981 he became the first American to finish one of the world's three big tours, the Giro, in which he was third best young rider.

He said: "It was generally considered impossible to enter or even race, and universally misunderstood by the entire American cycling establishment and press. I wanted to ride the Tour, but Italians generally must ride the Giro, and most riders can't do two big races a year, so a team needs to be fairly large to support both Tours as almost the entire team needs to be swapped out. The team I rode on, while first class, didn't budget for so many riders and so much travel, and they were all big pussies anyway, especially the so-called stars.

"I remember sprinting for a small mountain prime with Lucien van Impe. I almost burst out laughing because not one person I knew in the US would even believe me let alone comprehend how hard this all was, and here was one of my heroes that five years ago I couldn't dream of even meeting and here I was racing against him. 1981 had riders like van Impe and Gimondi in it so it was a real treat for me to race with these guys.

"My best day that year was on Tre Cime Di Lavaredo where I got fifth. It was insane. I have never seen crowds like that. Giovanni Battaglin had fitted his bike with a triple chainring up front and it was a good move. The steepness was madness. As I got to the last few kilometres the crowds grew intense. A sea of people parting before you the finish banner appears suddenly—above your head with a few hundred metres to go. Way above your head, and the seething crowd of *tifosi* makes it impossible to see the direction of the road at all. You have to literally watch for where they are parting to know what direction to go."

Mount retired in 1982, after seeing another gray hair every morning, as he put it. The following summer, Jonathan Boyer, a quiet and introspective vegetarian, slightly dandified as Geoffrey Nicholson described him, became the first American to ride the Tour de France. There is, incidentally, no love lost between Mount and Boyer, a personality clash. Boyer, too, came from California, although he was born in Utah. He studied as a veterinarian at the University of Colorado but was diverted after racing in Europe at eighteen, in the 1973 world junior championship. He rode to no great effect but his university plans dwindled and his cycling ambition flourished. He joined the AC Boulogne-Billancourt in a car-making suburb of northern Paris.

"Boulbi", as the area is called for short, is the city's most populous borough. The ACBB had a long been a nursery for professional teams—Stephen Roche, Robert Millar and Phil Anderson are among its English-speaking infants—and it remains the only club credited for winning the Tour de France. In 1962 Jacques Anquetil's St-Raphaël-Helyett team was registered as ACBB-St-Raphaël-Helyett because the manager, Mickey Weigant, was a member.

The ACBB started as the VC Billancourt in 1924 and through mergers with other clubs and sports became official sports club of Boulogne-Billancourt, run and financed by the council. Paul Weigant—Mickey was a nickname—ran its professional cycling team until the 1960s, after which he ran the amateur team the same way. The direction the best riders took thereafter was influenced by where Weigant had influence. When he worked with Peugeot, that was where most riders—including Roche, Millar and Anderson—turned professional.

The only rider in that group with which Boyer had some connection was Millar, for both were vegetarians. Probably the only vegetarians at that level, certainly in France. Their difference was that Boyer went not to Peugeot but Lejeune-BP. His sponsors were a Parisian bike firm run started in 1947 by two brothers, Roger and Marcel, and a multinational oil company. Unfortunately the bike company and not the petroleum giant put up the bulk of the cash. The man in charge was Henry Anglade, who came second in the 1959 Tour and who in 1960 led the race for two days. There, too, was Mount's idol, Lucien van Impe, reputed to ride the Tour only because his wife nagged him into it.

Boyer joined Lejeune-BP in 1977 to ride the Tour straight away—Lejeune didn't have many riders—but he crashed just before it started and then fell ill with a stomach virus. It took two years to recover. Proof he was over it came in the world championship in the shadow of Mont Blanc at Sallanches in eastern France in 1980. There was no secret that the circuit, which followed a valley, climbed the whopping hillside of Domency, returned, then climbed again and again, had been designed for Bernard Hinault. If that was true, nobody was disappointed. Hinault won in cold rain and only a handful finished. Among them, fifth, was Boyer.

At least two team managers took notice. Jean de Gribaldy, who was already Boyer's boss in the Sem team which he had joined after recovering, was watching from the stands. And somewhere else was Cyrille Guimard, Hinault's manager at Renault. There was no contest: Renault was one of the big beasts; de Gribaldy was good at inspiration but tightfisted with money. There was also pleasing symmetry because Boulogne-Billancourt, where Boyer started, was Renault's home town.

Félix Lévitan couldn't believe his luck. His race was in hard times. A French winner to coincide with the first finish on the Champs Élysées in 1975 was a patch on a threadbare coat. He could no longer get riders to take part. The field, around 130 since 1960, was 100 in 1977 and 110 in 1978. The first prize was no longer cash. From 30,000 francs it became a seaside apartment in 1976. The sponsor, Merlin-Plage, insisted it was worth three times as much, but that was Guy Merlin's estimation. If you didn't want a seaside apartment, or presumably if you took a cash offer, it was worth a lot less.

Lévitan needed fresh money. He had asked everyone he could ask. Those who agreed found their messages lost in the maelstrom of other people's commercials. There were so many sponsored competitions and jerseys that presentations were still going on after much of the audience had gone home. The sports minister was horrified as she watched the Tour finish on the Champs Élysées in 1981. Goddet said: "The young and pretty Edwige Avice was quite put out by the formalities of the ceremony, to the point that she mixed up the loudspeaker announcements and protested with great indignation that the organizers of the Tour had gone too far in announcing that 'The *Marseillaise* is brought to you by the real estate agent, Guy Merlin.' We had no end of trouble persuading her we wouldn't go that far!"

What greater dream, then, than to bring in American money, untapped wealth? And what more unbelievable than to find an American, however lowly, about to ride? Lévitan was so thrilled that he insisted Boyer abandon Renault's yellow and black for a stars-and-stripes champion's jersey to which he wasn't entitled. But, which he didn't refuse, because he had taken to calling himself "the American champion" after Sallanches.

It would be wrong to say he was the most reported rider when the Tour started in Nice on June 25. But he was good for stories, about his vegetarianism, how he had arrived with 50 kilograms of dried fruit, nuts and California dates, about the bucking bronco on the license plate of his American car, how he read the Bible every evening, about the little computer on his handlebars "that tells him how fast he is riding and how far he has ridden," how he had acupuncture treatment from a Korean doctor for his aching legs. He spoke good French, he was personable, and he was shrewd enough to wear a stetson when it suited.

"What made it hard to place Boyer, too," said Geoffrey Nicholson, "was not just that his career had been disrupted, but that it was now split between cycle-racing and his business interests as the European agent for American Grab-On accessories. That too he patiently explained. While he rode he did so with all his effort and concentration, but not simply to make money; he could earn more back home. He raced because he enjoyed it, and because it furthered his ambition to take professional cycling to the United States where he hoped to be involved in its promotion and maybe in television and journalism."

How far he rode—3,753 kilometres—was nowhere near as far as he took American cycling. By coming thirty-second in Paris he broke the bogey that, as Mount used to think, Europeans were supermen. He rode as a professional until 1987, riding Paris–Roubaix six times, the Giro three times and the Tour four more times, his best place twelfth in 1983.

Guimard described him as a *marginal*, not like the rest, not quite a hippie. Dennis Donovan of *Cycling* said English-speaking journalists felt sorry for him alone in a foreign land and offered him a bundle

of girlie mags. Boyer replied coldly: "No thank you, I have my Bible."
That earnestness made his downfall the more striking. He was jailed
for a year—he faced as many as 80—after ten charges in July 2002 of
"substantial sexual contact" with an underage girl in his church community. He left jail, worked in the cycle trade, then moved to Rwanda
as a coach.

2
Welcome To My World

The Tour winner hasn't always been alone. In 1984 two winners shared the podium: Laurent Fignon and an American riding with a club team, Marianne Martin. Fignon, who knows his mind, was not impressed by a woman who had ridden a quarter the distance, a lot more slowly and against riders of whom nobody but insiders had heard. He barely looked at her.

The women's Tour lasted a few years and struggled on as a separate promotion with around 60 riders. The other race that shared the road had a higher reputation. The Tour de l'Avenir—Tour of the Future— began in 1961 for amateurs and semiprofessionals riding for their country. It preceded the professionals on mountain stages and, in the admittedly biased view of its director, the journalist René de Latour, had better racing. Its winner in 1964, Felice Gimondi, won the main Tour the following year.

The purpose was to bring in money but also to interest countries such as the Soviet Union which had no professionals. The Avenir changed over the years, in name, route and riders and now has little connection with the original. But the idea lived on and, without warning during the rest day at Cancale in Brittany, Lévitan said the following year's Tour de France—1983—would also be open to amateurs. Legally, it was startling because cycling was still amateur and professional along with other Olympic sports. It had the same rules that troubled the British back in the days of George Mills, that an amateur who raced with professionals became a professional himself. But it followed the Tour's dreams of *mondialisation*.

Goddet's favorite sport was rugby, which he learned in England. He was also a soccer fan. In 1955 he and one of his soccer reporters, the former international Gabriel Hanot, had been upset by boasts that Wolverhampton Wanderers of England were "champions of the world" because they had won friendlies with clubs on the Continent. "Let Wolverhampton Wanderers go to Moscow and Budapest," Hanot wrote. The two then offered a European Cup in 1955 to find a European if not a world champion. Goddet always regretted that neither thought to copyright or lay legal claim to it. Soccer's administration took it over.

Goddet watched enviously, therefore, as the still more adventurous World Cup played out in Madrid, Spain, in 1982. He was impressed but disturbed that all he heard on television sets turned loud in Switzerland, where that summer's Tour started, was soccer. Even his own newspaper gave more space to it than to cycling. The two most televised sports events—the Olympics and the World Cup—are every four years. The Tour could copy, Goddet reasoned. Every year after the Games, it would open to amateurs from the communist bloc and from the USA, Canada, Colombia and Africa. A world cup, small letters, of cycling.

There had been hints of *mondialisation* before. An African team rode in 1950, and on the same day, two of its riders provided the Tour's most colorful tale. On July 28, 1950, France was in a heat wave as the Tour set off from Perpignan for Nîmes. The bunch was not inclined to race and, near St-Tropez, ran into the sea. The only riders untroubled by the heat were the six representing North Africa, particularly what was then the French *département* of Algeria. Marcel Molinès and Abdel-Khader Zaaf, billed as the Lion of Chabli after his home town, raced off together. They gathered enough lead to make Zaaf the probable *maillot jaune*. They had fifteen kilometres to go when Zaaf started zigzagging, stopped and fell asleep under a tree. Molinès went on to win the stage, still the only black rider to win one.

Zaaf woke up a few minutes later, got on his bike and rode off the wrong way. Spectators called an ambulance and Zaaf's Tour came to an end. Legend says the spectators revived him with wine to which Zaaf, presumed to be a Muslim, was unaccustomed. It went to his head and in drunken confusion he parted in the direction he had come. There's no doubt about falling asleep under a tree. Plenty of pictures show that. The alcohol story is improbable. Few people like wine when they first taste it. Would Zaaf, if a Muslim, have drunk enough to make him drunk before he realized he was offending religious law? And how much wine would even a dedicated boozer need to ride off the wrong way? "In those days," says Jean-Pierre Ollivier, "people didn't speak of doping."

Molinès won and vanished from Tour history after stage eighteen. He would now be nearly 90—he was born in December 1928—but nothing has been heard of him since he stopped racing in 1953. Zaaf, on the other hand, got thrown into jail. He returned to Algeria with money he hadn't thought to declare and the police came looking for him. There was a dispute and he was shot in the leg. He too then vanished. But in 1982 a fan recognized an old man leaving a train in Paris. He had come for an eye operation demanded by his diabetes. He said he had been jailed for two years without trial, that he had lost almost all he owned. It made him a greater celebrity than ever, especially since France was struggling with its conscience after the Algerian war of independence. Flowers, telegrams and gifts came from all over the country. He died four years later, a forgotten man once more remembered.

More than introducing new countries and bringing back old ones, the post-Olympic Tour was to spend only nine or ten days in France. The rest it would pass in France's eight neighboring countries, perhaps even cross to Britain or go up to Holland. The first foreign start was in Holland, in Amsterdam in 1954. That had been done, the Tour veteran Jock Wadley surmised, as a spoiler for the fledgling Tour of Europe promoted by Jean Leulliot. He was the man, you remember, who ran a chaotic substitute Tour for the Germans. The Tour of Europe didn't last much longer.

More than that, though, the post-Olympic Tour could start in America. Lévitan never let go of his fascination with the place and there was talk of dropping the flag at the White House. Goddet remained keen long after he had retired. "I envisaged starting the 2000 Tour de France in New York, but unfortunately the organizers were afraid of the strain that this would put on riders and staff," he said.

Journalists were baffled. There was the "Why?" But there was also "How?" Concorde would reduce travel time but it wouldn't change jet lag. And Concorde held 120 passengers at most. There were only fourteen around the world, most on scheduled services, and getting enough on the same route on the same day—a one-way charter there and another back a week later—looked improbable. It had also been a struggle just to get to Britain. In 1974, Lévitan was persuaded to visit Plymouth so Brittany farmers could sell artichokes there. The farmers, tired of taking their crop to the Channel ports, started their own ferry to Plymouth. The Tour was paid to spend a day in southwest England, riding up and down an unopened bypass. The riders resented the journey and rode all day in a sullen mob. Little of the advertising caravan went, having no market in Britain. Customs delayed the bikes because rules allowed only one each, and entertaining word spread that Goddet forgot his passport and was followed all day by a policeman.

The race was so dull and spectators so few compared to predictions that the mass-circulation *Daily Mirror* asked: TOUR DE FRANCE: CAN 40 MILLION FRENCHMEN BE WRONG?

The Atlantic air link never happened and, the last Concorde having flown in 2003, it now looks even more unlikely. The Tour needed dreamers like Lévitan but it also needed younger men, men who didn't sell epic schemes like goldfish at a fun fair.

Goddet and Lévitan referred to each other as *"mon chèr Jacques"* and *"mon chèr Félix"* in public but their private spats were bitter. Lévitan was jealous of how the Tour had dropped into Goddet's lap be-

A memorial to Jacques Goddet on the Tourmalet. It was unveiled shortly after his death in 2000.

cause he was Victor Goddet's son. "He believed," said Goddet, "that it stopped his taking first position in areas in which we worked together. I admit that connections gave me an advantage but I shouldn't have kept it had I not been able to do the job. It was also clear that my social position was more established from birth [Lévitan was the son of a shopkeeper, Goddet the son of the businessman who owned the Tour, bike tracks and a national newspaper]. And I understand that Félix, supported by a wife, Geneviève—the only wife he had, which shows the links that bound them [Goddet married four times]—who strongly admired her husband and pushed him with all the force of her affection to the top, constantly wanted to level the differences."

Lévitan's inferiority complex showed in amusing ways. Goddet loved fancy cars and so Lévitan bought a Jaguar. But, because he and Geneviève spoke no English, he stuck French translations on the dashboard above the heater, the choke and the lights. When Goddet stood for election as mayor of St-Tropez in 1965, Lévitan stood at Rambouillet. In this case Lévitan came out better: he was elected and Goddet wasn't.

He wasn't above overruling officials when they decided the "wrong" way. He was a Godfather, said the British rider, Barry Hoban, "and he used to overrule the commissaires. The race director, theoretically, has no control over the race. Once the race is in progress, the commissaires are the ones who should define what happens, if someone infringes a rule. But Lévitan used to just overrule them."

In 1968 Lévitan produced the rare achievement of making journalists on the Tour go on strike. That year, following Simpson's death, was to be the Tour of Health, symbolically starting in Vittel, a town in the Vosges mountains known for the spring water it bottled. Whether the supposed clampdown on drugs was the reason or not, it turned out a dull Tour. The long, flat stages into the wind ended day after day in a sprint. The reporters said so and, at least privately, grew nostalgic for an era just passed in which riders dosed themselves with whatever they wanted.

Lévitan accused them on television of watching "with tired eyes." He entered the press room at Bordeaux to have it out with Jean Leulliot, among the critics. Leulliot reported the encounter in *Sud Ouest*, the regional daily. "What gives you the right?" Lévitan demanded. "It has nothing to do with you. You're here to put up and to shut up, and don't forget it. The Tour is a god and it should be venerated like one."

Leulliot, for all his black points, was a respected veteran. He had followed 27 Tours and suffered in the process, cracking his skull and breaking a leg and a collarbone in a crash. For fellow reporters, this was one criticism too many. They weren't going to be told their job and they weren't going to be turned into public relations writers churning out bland and obsequious copy that hid the truth. They went on strike next day and refused to report the stage to Labouheyre. They jeered at Lévitan, put on dark glasses and held banners saying "Riders, beware! Tired eyes are watching you!"

Next day, tragically now, reporters were back in the news. Two of them, riding motorcycles, tangled up with each other at St-Aubin-de-Blaye and plowed into the crowd, injuring eleven.

It was Lévitan who wanted the Tour to go back to sponsored teams, Lévitan who wanted to bring in amateurs, and Lévitan who saw the potential of American cycling and American money. And it cost him his job.

Lévitan was Émilien Amaury's man. Amaury was stubborn and could be pitiless but he was loyal to Lévitan—more than to his own son, Philippe. French law doesn't allow wills of the sort familiar in Anglo-Saxon countries. Children must inherit all and inherit equally. That was of no concern to Amaury, who left almost everything to his daughter, Françine. It took lawyers six years to sort out, after which Philippe owned Amaury's daily papers and his sister the monthlies.

In 1986, Goddet was 81 and said he would retire. In 1987, Lévitan went as well, but not of his choice. Philippe Amaury fired him. Without speaking to Goddet or Amaury, Lévitan had arranged for American television rights for the Tour to be paid to an intermediary, Philippe Riquois, a former business colleague of Bernard Hinault. Riquois was president of Broadcasting Rights International, which handled television rights to the Tour outside the European Broadcasting Union. His introduction to the Tour had been Louison Bobet, who commissioned him to find sites in the USA for the sea-treatment spas he ran in retirement. Seeing further chances, Riquois ran an American version of the Tour in 1983.

The race took place over four days on the east coast but ran up losses of $500,000. Lévitan gave Riquois the US television rights to wipe out his debts. And when he arrived at work on March 17, 1987, he found a lawyer waiting and the lock to his office changed. Goddet was also there. Lévitan's office was searched and he was dismissed and sent out of the building. A week later the Tour said there had been "serious divergence in the group's strategy" and accused Lévitan of being "too personal and deliberately secretive" in his business dealings.

Lévitan denied misdoing. Émilien Amaury had told him to do it, he said, and it wasn't for him to question why or how. A long legal tussle followed and he went off for a long sulk by the Mediterranean. A fellow journalist remembers that Lévitan came to see him. The phone rang as they talked and the journalist apologized. "Please," Lévitan said, "I know what it's like when the phone never rings any more." He stayed away from the Tour until a surprise appearance in 1998, when he said only that he and the Amaury organization had "come to an understanding." But he never again spoke of the Tour de France.

In the end barely anything remained of his dream. The communist countries backed out because of a missile crisis between west and east and because the west had stayed away from the Moscow Olympics three years earlier; the western sponsors were cross; only the Colombians turned up. They brought talented riders, of which Lucho Herrera was the best, and the noisiest TV and radio commentators European journalism has known. Then towards the end of the millennium the distinction between amateurs and professionals was abandoned anyway.

3

Mr Smiley, Mr Grumpy, Mr Cheat

There is a link between George Mount, who developed America's Grand Tour dreams, and Greg LeMond, who made them flourish. Mount and a tall man with a floppy mustache, John Howard, were racing in the Sierra mountains which separate California from the rest of America. They had turned the event into a two-man tussle. Driving on the same road was Bob LeMond and his teenage son, a thin and spotty boy with braces on his teeth. They followed Mount and Howard over Mount Rose and then down the descent. LeMond shoved the accelerator and braked until the tires squealed to keep up with them. He couldn't. The boy thought it the coolest thing in the world, to use the phrase of the era, that his father couldn't keep up with guys on bicycles.

LeMond Junior first went to Europe in 1978. He was thrilled to meet his childhood hero, Jean-Claude Killy. The Frenchman had won three golds at the Olympics in 1968. LeMond was only six and dreamed of skiing, not cycling. Now he could ride beside his hero, a teenager out for a bike trip with a 35-year-old international hero. LeMond wasn't yet an international hero and Killy wasn't yet president of the company behind the Tour de France. Neither knowing where the future lay, they rode around the ski resort of Morzine on the day the Tour passed.

"It was the first time I'd seen professional cyclists," LeMond said. "They were demigods. I wouldn't go as far as saying that I said to myself 'One day you'll ride this road with the Tour' but what I can say is that in 1984 that's just what I did."

Greg LeMond took over where Boyer left off. The difference isn't that LeMond won and Boyer didn't. But Boyer was the ground breaker. It is harder to lead than follow. It is harder to pioneer when nobody notices. "The average European would recognize Boyer's name before the average American," says Ed Pavelka, editor of *Bicycling* and then of roadbikerider.com. "Those of us in cycling were in awe, but that's about as far as it went for his celebrity."

Where Boyer had been pleasant but serious, LeMond delighted. His whoop when he realized he had beaten Laurent Fignon in the last seconds to win the Tour made Frenchmen happier for him than sorry for Fignon. There was delight when LeMond and his wife Kathy were pictured in bed, an American flag as blanket, sipping champagne. Hearts melted when, recovering from shotgun wounds, he returned with much-improved French and a delicious drawling American accent.

Goddet said: "I was so happy that an American won, especially Greg—who was a really nice, intelligent guy [and] I think that Armstrong's victory this year [1999] is perhaps the most extraordinary event in the history of the Tour—the fact that a Tour winner has triumphed over an evil such as cancer will go down in human history. It was a delight, especially after the succession of horrible doping stories."

The problem was that Armstrong *was* subsequently condemned for doping. And where LeMond pleased everyone—Fignon branded him a hypocrite who'd go to any length not to rub people up the wrong way—Armstrong seemed ill at ease with the world, and a profiteering adventurer who knew nothing of the sport's legends. He was "arrogant and brash," said Jeremy Whittle at *Procycling*.

To win the Tour seven times, to have a break and then try again, risked attracting comment, as Lady Bracknell put it. His progress from cancer to winning the Tour was the most wonderful fairy tale in history, said LeMond, or it was something else. The bitterness between them showed when they shared a stage in Paris: their backs were permanently lightly turned to each other. Like Fignon and Martin. And time showed LeMond to be right: Armstrong was forced into admitting what an investigation called the biggest doping scheme in history.

It wasn't the first time LeMond had fallen out with an American. He and Boyer were in the same Renault team. "They didn't get on," said Jean-Luc Gatellier in *Vélo*. The two rode the world championship at Goodwood, a horse racing town in southern England, in 1982. Boyer broke clear in the last miles and, because LeMond, Sean Kelly and Beppe Saronni were all too nervous to make a move which could favor a rival, it looked possible he could stay away. The risk wasn't enormous but it was too great for LeMond, who went off in chase of his own teammate. Pictures show Saronni smiling as he spots the stalemate has been broken. The group overtook Boyer and neither he nor LeMond won. The victory went to Saronni.

Boyer was predictably furious. LeMond was calm. "This US team was not a team at all," he said. "I didn't stay with the other riders or spend time with them, and I paid my own way to the worlds. I was definitely not going to give up my chances for someone who would never do the same for me." Boyer learned the lesson. In the following year's Tour, said Gatellier, Boyer's view was that "I'm an individualist, I'm American, the only American in this Tour de France, and I have to think of my own performance."

Lance Armstrong was an icon in America. Alain Gallopin, a former French rider who worked with his team, once remarked publicly that the American barely acknowledged him one morning. The sky fell on him. "I learned that, in America, you never, ever make the slightest criticism," he said.

Armstrong—in the USA he is referred to by his first name, in Europe by his last—insisted throughout that he was clean and that he had never been penalized for drug-taking. But he did have a positive finding in his first Tour and, later, *L'Équipe* published pages of cross-referenced documents which it said proved he had used the blood-improving drug, EPO. The positive finding was in 1999, when *L'Équipe* said he had been tested fifteen times and found clear fourteen times. The remaining test showed he had taken corticoids, synthetically produced hormones which reduce pain and fatigue. They were banned in 1980 but detection was perfected only days before Armstrong's test. His team doctor, Luis Del Moral, gave judges a prescription saying Armstrong needed cortisone and, although the rules said prescriptions were to be shown before and not after a test, the amounts were small and Armstrong escaped sanction.

His subsequent tests were also clear—twelve in 2000, ten in 2001, nine in 2002 and 2003, eight in 2004, according to figures *L'Équipe* said came from the UCI. Throughout this time Armstrong denied taking drugs. A French and an Irish journalist, Pierre Ballester and David Walsh, wrote a book which cast doubt on that claim. "Extraordinary allegations need extraordinary proof," Armstrong retaliated.

On August 23, 2005, *L'Équipe* filled half its broadsheet pages with that proof, that Armstrong had also taken EPO in 1999.

The dope-testing agency at Châtenay-Malabry, near Paris, had kept urine collected that year. Without it, it had no material with which to work on test procedures. EPO was banned as corticoids had been banned, but there was no way to show its presence. Then in 2001 *Nature* published research by Françoise Lasne and Jacques de Ceaurriz showing a successful test. It was used in the Olympic Games in 2000 and the Tour de France in 2001.

De Ceaurriz worked on samples identified only by number. He felt no mission to clean up sport, he told *Le Monde*. "There's no feeling in the laboratory of conducting a battle," he said. "We're professionals." It was scientific research.

Each rider received a numbered bottle at his test and each number was noted against a name. The names and numbers were at UCI headquarters in Switzerland. The results from the lab, all negative in 1999, went to the Ministry of Sport and Youth in Paris and to the World Anti-Doping Agency, created that year.

Damien Ressiot had worked at *L'Équipe* since 1990. He reported soccer, grew bored, took the chance to work on the dope stories that Ballester had reported before being fired. He was moved by Armstrong's challenge to find "extraordinary proof" and, from December 2004, set out to look. He was on the edge of his fortieth birthday when he thought he'd found it. Ressiot, like any journalist, protects his sources. He won't say how he knew retrospective tests had been carried out nor that twelve of the seventy samples were positive. But he knew the race leader is always tested and he knew how many days Armstrong led the race. Fifteen of the seventy retested samples must have been Armstrong's.

The UCI says Ressiot asked to see a confidential file, as the journalist Daniel Friebe put it, to "write an article which celebrated Armstrong's career." Ressiot may have a different version. What seems agreed is that the UCI asked Armstrong and that Armstrong agreed. Ressiot copied the file and it was one of many printed in *L'Équipe* on August 23, 2005, under the front page headline *Le Mensonge Armstrong*: the Armstrong lie. Against test 185557 were three red bars. They showed, Ressiot said, a positive test for synthetic EPO. The paper published five more results—Ressiot won't say where they came from—with red bars.

It printed forms signed by Armstrong which showed, the paper said, the tests were his.

Armstrong protested, inaccurately called *L'Équipe* a "tabloid" with the suggestion that it was a scandal rag, deplored how the story had been obtained, but took no legal action. The UCI said it would do nothing because the tests weren't conducted in the Tour, that it had been deceived, that de Ceaurriz had never said the tests were being carried out. The row rumbled on, more and more introspective, until Sylvia Schenk of the German cycling federation said the UCI "seemed less interested in the resolution of the Armstrong doping case than they are in finding the leak."

That allegation lived on in a way Schenk couldn't have suspected. The stories around Armstrong grew more and more numerous, supplied largely by riders he had snubbed and who took their moment of cold revenge. Among them were Frankie Andreu, Tyler Hamilton and Floyd Landis, each of whom held grudges against Armstrong and testified to a national inquiry. In January, 2013, with court cases mounting and investigators coming closer, Armstrong surrendered. Oprah Winfrey, an American celebrity with her own television station, asked Armstrong a succession of questions to which he answered Yes. The man branded the biggest dope cheat in history had finally told the truth.

What made Schenk's comment the more relevant is that attention then focused on the *Union Cycliste Internationale* itself. Its head at the time, a pugnacious Dutchman called Hein Verbruggen, repeatedly denied and still denies that he or the UCI knew of Armstrong's cheating and stayed silent at best or cooperated at worst. But a new man took over when Verbruggen left. And Brian Cookson began an inquiry which included examining the hard disks of all the UCI's computers.

What gave the story a further twist was that no sooner had Armstrong left cycling for a rest, a clumsy-looking ginger-haired American with a bad hip took over as winner. He wasn't the winner for long. It had been a century since Maurice Garin had been the first—only—winner of the Tour de France to be disqualified and now Floyd Landis joined him.

One day in that Tour, Landis lost ten minutes and the next he rode so well that he led the field in by six minutes.

The computer at Châtenay was subsequently broken into and doctored files produced to cast doubts on his guilt. But there was no doubt.

He became the only winner of the Tour de France who can't watch the race from the roadside without being arrested. There is a warrant out for him in France so that police can question him. Stéphane Mandard wrote in *Le Monde*: "Landis launched himself into a huge campaign to denigrate the laboratory. A battalion of lawyers at his elbow, he contested his positive test for testosterone. In May 2007, Jacques de Ceaurriz, who rarely left his office, had to spend six days in Malibu, California, to defend the laboratory's dossier in a procedure launched against the rider by the American anti-doping agency. He brought off a sparkling victory."

De Ceaurriz had been head of Châtenay-Malabry since 1997 and director of analyses for the French anti-doping agency since 2007. *Le Monde* said he brought dope-testing out of the prehistoric age. His laboratory had greater success than any other in finding cheats. His work perfected the test for corticoids and he was working on ways to detect blood transfusions. His death at age 60 in January 2010 brought an immediate tribute from French athletics. But nothing from cycling.

Part six: L'arrivée

The "arrivée" is the finish, one kilometre beyond the red triangle above the road. Whatever has happened all day, the rewards and the losses will be there. Everything that went before now makes sense or has to be explained. Nothing is certain before the "ligne d'arrivée", what the Dutch called the "eindstreep" and English-speakers simply "the line".

1
Into The Future...

The year that Félix Lévitan brought in his amateurs, Lucho Herrera and his men of the mountains brought fun and excitement—but they didn't come back for another go. They left a curious legacy, however, for which they've never been thanked. Colombia is a long way from France and evening in one is noon in the other. When the Colombians got to their hotel, they wanted to call home. A reporter called Jean-Marie Leblanc saw them outside a call box, coins in hand, and one of the first things he did on becoming organizer was demand every rider have a phone in his room.

Leblanc followed the tradition of journalists running the race. The only exception was the transition between Lévitan's firing and Leblanc's arrival in 1989. For the two intermediate years the race was run by a muddled committee, a combination of the unknown businessman Jean-François Naquet-Radiguet and a longtime lieutenant of the Tour, Xavier Louy. Naquet-Radiguet was replaced after a year by a former tennis player, Jean-Pierre Courcol, a director of the Société, and then finally permanence was established.

Leblanc had ridden the Tour, finishing in lowly positions in 1968 and 1970. In the second he had the distinction of being fined for picnicking. His Bic team, sponsored by a company making lighters and ballpoint pens, arranged it for publicity. Leblanc, Luis Ocaña and Jan Janssen were fined $6 for accepting food outside a feeding area.

Leblanc is from northern France, one of 650 people at Fontaine-au-Bois, a village southeast of Arras near the Belgian border, where he became deputy mayor. His father raced before the second world war. Leblanc himself rode his first race at seventeen in 1961 and won his first at Bousies in May next year. "I started racing seriously fairly late because my father forbade me to race until it was clear I was going to continue my studies. I was in a club, yes, but there was no coach, no adviser. Nobody even told me I shouldn't wear underpants under my shorts, so I rode with those on and with the chamois in my shorts. All I knew was what I'd learned from reading Louison Bobet's book, *Champion Cycliste*."

After studying law and economics at university in Lille for two years and then dropping out, he supported himself by delivering chocolates for a local factory before becoming a professional cyclist in 1966. The first time he saw the Tour was when he rode it. Until then he had followed it only on the radio and through the magazines *Miroir Sprint* and *Miroir des Sports* that his father brought home every July. "I was just a little rider," he said. "Against riders like Simpson, like Merckx, like Ocaña in the same bunch as me, I'm obliged to say that I lacked class."

One day at the start of the Tour de l'Hérault near the French Mediterranean coast, he was sitting on a bench when he noticed the rider beside him was Simpson. And Simpson chatted to him. "Can you imagine that? You're a little rider and the world professional champion, with the rainbow jersey on his shoulders, starts chatting to you as a friend. Unforgettable!"

Years later, by then director of the Tour, he had a call from an even greater champion: Eddy Merckx. "'Sir', he called me. I interrupted him. 'Eddy, please, don't call me sir; I was just a simple rider. You were there, big guy.'"

Leblanc had seven wins as a professional, rode the Tour twice and Paris–Roubaix five times. He retired at the end of 1970. That year he told *L'Équipe*: "In France there are a dozen professional riders who make a good living, that's to say 5,000 francs a month and more. Then there are another 30 or so who make a reasonable living, between 2,500 and 3,000 francs a month. And a third category, alas, almost on the minimum wage. I have the luck to be in the second group. I've always loved cycling madly, to the point of giving up a life that would be quieter and certainly better paid."

And that was the life he went to, quieter and better paid. He joined *La Voix du Nord*, a regional daily, in 1971 and six years later moved to Paris as chief cycling correspondent of *L'Équipe* and editor of its monthly, *Vélo*. From there he took over the Tour. His first job was to undo the muddle inherited from Lévitan. Out went the five-dollar sponsors, replaced by fewer but bigger "partners", as they were now known.

"My first preoccupation has been to restore the Tour's sporting credibility," he said. "We have simplified the Tour, which had become incomprehensible to the public, and cut the trophies from twelve to six, with just four classifications: the yellow jersey, the winner of the stage, the polka dot jersey for the best climber, and the green jersey for the points competition. And sponsors have returned. Cutting the number of *partenaires* has increased their visibility, which means we can charge them higher prices."

The Tour became a separate part of Philippe Amaury's ganglion organization. The organizer no longer also worked at *L'Équipe*, full or part time. The Tour had moved to a white, modern building outside

Jean-Marie LeBlanc in 1997.

the Paris ring-road, at Issy-les-Moulineaux. Not only did it and its founding newspaper occupy separate buildings but the bridge that linked them was removed. To go from one to the other means walking in the rain.

Leblanc sat in the building on the right as you see it from the street. Not only the Tour was different. So was management style. Once a month, around 8pm, Leblanc cleared the desks and moved the chairs and brought in his friends: Philippe Sudres on saxophone, Bernard on banjo, Patrick on drums and often a pianist, a double-bass player and a trumpeter. Leblanc took his clarinet from its case and the friends threw themselves into a *boeuf*—a musical jam.

No bad player, Leblanc: in June 2008 he played Mozart's clarinet concerto with the *Salle Philharmonique du Conservatoire de Liège*, across in Belgium. He and his office musicians weren't shy about playing in the street on France's national music day. Florian Joyard, who saw them, said Leblanc "wasn't the least engaged of them—you just have to see him tapping his feet, eyes closed, blowing into his instrument, launched now into a solo in *Brave Margot*, then raising it towards the sax player, his whole body moving to the music to the point of breathlessness."

Leblanc's first Tour as organizer was the closest. All depended on the time-trial into Paris. Laurent Fignon could win or Greg LeMond could overtake him. Even they couldn't call it. LeMond won by eight seconds, the lowest margin ever. The picture of his openmouthed joy as he hears the news has become one of the best known images of the Tour. Leblanc's worst Tour was when he sent Richard Virenque home in 1998, the year in which police took over where cycling's officials had proved ineffective and uncovered mass doping in the Tour generally and Virenque's team specifically. Leblanc sent home the whole Festina team a few days after its Belgian soigneur, Willy Voet, was caught driving a carload of drugs en route for the Tour.

"It was essential for the credibility of the Tour," Leblanc said. "We couldn't carry on accepting a team, even the best team of the moment whose leader was the darling of France, when it had just been attested that it was doping itself. It wasn't possible. And I, a man, when Virenque took me in his arms, crying, I was on the edge of crying as well. I didn't expel the team for the joy of my heart. I'm not a tyrant. I have nothing against Virenque or against his team. Quite the contrary.

"I remember how, a month before, I had been with Madame Chirac [wife of the president, Jacques Chirac] in the Corrèze, where the Tour's first time-trial was to be. We came across the Festina team. I said to Mme Chirac: 'Look what an exemplary team they are; the riders are learning the course, like true professionals.'"

2

...Darkly

Leblanc's friendship with Jacques and Bernardette Chirac is one of many intriguing strands in the Tour's darkest moment. There had been dramas before—Malléjac, Simpson—and there had been fruitless fresh starts, like the Tour of Health and its Vittel mineral water in 1968. What's become known as the Festina scandal of 1988 showed nothing had changed except for the worse. And, that behind it could have been a mix of determination and revenge at the very top of France.

The preliminaries are short enough: a balding Belgian whose background as a bus driver had made him an expert on sports medicine was driving a stash of drugs in a new Fiat. Willy Voet was crossing from Belgium into France on July 8 when Customs stopped him. That was unusual because border formalities had long been dropped across much of Europe.

Voet's more probable route was the main highway from Belgium to the French ferry port of Calais, where he had booked to England and on from there to the start of the Tour in Ireland. Instead he turned on to a minor road to the Belgian village of Dronkaard. He says he doesn't know why. This improbable route added an hour to his journey. Equally improbable was that at 6:30 on a Tuesday morning there would be a "routine check" by French border police. The stash in red and blue bags behind the back seat was easy to find. There was enough to get a whole team through the Tour. It's easy to imagine the smirk as police asked Voet if he had a prescription. There are few limits to what can be taken across borders but drugs and medicines are exceptions. Tragedy turned to farce when Voet was ordered to strip and more drugs fell from his underpants.

France's sports minister, Marie-George Buffet, was in Dublin. Bruno Roussel, Festina's manager, said she gave him a knowing smile. "She already knew all about the arrest, the analyses and everything else." Roussel engaged a lawyer, Bertrand Lavelot, who defended riders in doping cases. "The whole thing stinks," Lavelot said. "It's part of a political battle between the Left and Right."

Roussel says now that Festina's downfall began not on the Belgian border but in April, when Agnès Pierret, administration director of the Tour, asked if Bernardette Chirac could watch Festina try the time-trial course in her home region southeast of Limoges. Her husband Jacques was a politician of the right. He had been elected president without an administrative majority and was obliged to appoint a prime minister from the left. Lionel Jospin in turn didn't have enough support to form a cabinet and he had to take on a communist as sports minister. That was Marie-George Buffet. Far from lying low, she went through the files and found a lot undone. She wrote her own doping laws and brought in tighter controls on the Tour.

Now Bernardette Chirac…

Roussel took the call from Agnès Pierret and protested that Bernardette Chirac and a load of reporters would get in the way. Then Jean-Marie Leblanc came on the line and begged him to agree, saying this was Festina's year, that Virenque could win for France. Roussel backed down and helped the TV crews. Bernardette Chirac pointed out every monument, every model farm, every grazing cow and decried the scandalous lack of investment by the prime minister, Lionel Jospin.

The film was to be broadcast on July 18. It never was. July 18 was when, in the back of the Chez Gillou café in the Corrèze, Leblanc threw Virenque and his team out of the Tour. According to testimony at the trial, Jacques Chirac called Virenque, sympathizing and asking him to accept the decision. Leblanc spent that night with Jacques and Bernardette Chirac at their château.

Catching a soigneur in a drug-laden car was a superb chance to push the changes that Marie-George Buffet wanted. It also exposed the laxity of the previous right-wing government. Hotels and team cars were searched and teams went home, disqualified or in protest. Riders, officials and soigneurs were arrested and some were charged. Some confessed. Virenque insisted tearfully he was innocent until, confronted in court in Lille by questioning less obsequious than that of cycling reporters, he broke down. *"Oui, je me suis dopé,"* he said—"Yes, I took drugs."

While others stared at cell doors, Roussel tried to work out why it had happened. He had dinner with a policeman in the case. They had gotten to know each other. Roussel asked if Voet had been *balancé* (thrown to the lions) by an insider, someone within cycling. "You understand I can't really tell you," the policeman said. Roussel mentioned a name, which he hasn't repeated. The policeman said: "I can't confirm that." But with a smile—and without denying it.

Hein Verbruggen, the head of the UCI, said Voet and Festina were already suspect. The theory—unproved—was that a source within cycling tipped off Belgian police. That may have had the support of the French sports ministry. With that backing, Belgian police may have followed Voet until he approached the border, at which point carrying drugs without prescription would become illegal. Either Voet knew which route he would take, or police had been ordered to all likely points, or police tailing Voet had reported his route. The rest followed and explains Roussel's impression that Buffet already knew about the arrest.

But it is a supposition that will never be confirmed or denied. He has never named the name he mentioned to his policeman friend. However, the idea that police were waiting by chance, at 6:30am, on a country road so minor that it isn't even colored on the road atlas, needs to be explained.

Roussel had reason to concoct a theory that shifted the blame. During the investigation he came over as a weak man who left the drugs side of the team to the doctor, who in turn failed to keep it to the mild level he favored. Roussel had reason to lessen the blame that fell on him but the most profitable time would have been during the inquiry. Yet it wasn't until 2001, three years later, that he explained his theory. By then he had left cycling to work for a building company. He now lectures young cyclists and their clubs on the danger and futility of taking drugs.

Willy Voet was ruled *persona non grata* by the Tour and he too left the sport, going back to bus-driving. Marie-George Buffet lost her job in the 2002 election, when the country swung behind Jacques Chirac. But her laws remain on the book and she is still on the far left of politics.

The Festina scandal left a heavy mark on Leblanc. He aged visibly, said the reporter William Fotheringham. For a while Leblanc considered allowing only riders of less than 25, getting rid of old riders and old habits, confident that within days people would recognize the new *maillot jaune*, the new stars. But the mood passed and the UCI's and then the French government's greater control of blood doping, and the prospect of a trustworthy test for EPO, reassured him.

"I was overwhelmed, wounded," he recalled. "Between 1998 and 2006, I tried hard to change the sport. I spent whole evenings alone in my office, reading books, trying to write the ten commandments of the ethical charter, only to face a whole new set of scandals. It's as if the riders in general had just said…" He paused, prepared to raise a forearm abruptly in rude salute and said "pardon the gesture I'm about to make…"

3
The Lone Star State

The story of Lance Armstrong the "cancer survivor" never ran in France as it did in America. Gilles Comte, editor of *Vélo*, said: "Armstrong won his first Tour de France in 1999, and the Texan's performance suffered from the Festina affair which broke a year earlier and which had left cycling badly bruised. The harm was all the greater because Armstrong had recovered from cancer, which brought him the status of hero across the Atlantic but that of a dubious champion in France. The story of 'cancer survivor' doesn't work with us. People referred to a 'miracle' in a way that showed their suspicion."

Armstrong "trained harder than everyone else", said his publicity. Some accepted it. Others asked who trained second hardest. Without knowing or explaining that, the claim had no value. Nor did his reputation for being first to ride the Tour's mountains before the race, to learn their ways. Most, it's true, didn't. But many did, among them Lucien van Impe, who won the mountains prize six times in ten years and pointed out his precedence abruptly. He didn't care to be made out careless in his professionalism.

In 2001 journalists on the Tour accorded Armstrong their *Prix Citron*, the lemon award for the most sour-faced rider in the race. In 2002 spectators shouted "Drugged! Drugged!" so often as he passed that he said he'd be rich if he had a dollar for each. In 2003 the White House rounded on France for being among nations not joining the USA in invading Iraq. E-mail cartoons denigrating French life, myths and supposed cowardice were traced to the USA. The president, George Bush, was already unpopular in France and became even more so. Armstrong was a Texan, he called himself Bush's friend, and the combination didn't help. Word spread that his life was threatened and police followed him in the Tour.

The contradiction is that Armstrong tried to please. It's true that he said the Tour was a race and not a personality contest, but he did try. He has never spoken good French. That didn't trouble the French because they appreciate anyone giving it a go, however clumsily. Armstrong, who didn't like speaking French, was once questioned in English on Eurosport channel and answered in French regardless, to show willingness. The interviewer had to ask him to stick to English because French translators weren't standing by.

And yet despite that, he undid everything by what France saw as rash and sometimes crude and now and then easily disproved statements. *L'Équipe*, when it printed its EPO allegations, was called a tabloid. It isn't. It's neither tabloid in shape nor style. He said dope-testers in the Tour had hauled him from his bed before dawn when there were witnesses to say that they hadn't. He said during the ESPY Awards in America that all the French soccer team had tested positive "…as assholes." He claimed he had had more dope tests than the records showed.

France, regardless of the stories that ran in America, didn't hate him. It was suspicious, yes, and spectators were as crude and outspoken as Armstrong himself. But come what may, the man won seven Tours. Come what may, they add, "if he *did* take something then it's no more than cyclists have always done."

But contradictions follow him. In 2005, his last Tour before his comeback, the Tour conducted a survey of spectators along the Champs Élysées. "There were more Americans than any other spectators," Leblanc said. Whether he meant more Americans than other foreigners, or whether he really did mean just that—that more than one in two was American—it demonstrates the grip that Armstrong had.

And there were more contradictions. His comeback in 2009 was greeted with dismay. He belonged to the past, a not always salubrious past, and his domination had been admired but not loved. He won every year in the same way, it was said, because the others were too overawed to attack him. Then indifference turned to interest and finally enthusiasm. If he could win seven times in a row, retire and think about doing it all over at nearly 40, this was a man above others. And in Monaco fans beside the road were twice as numerous as usual, just to see him.

Then, as if to reverse everything, came a civil war within Armstrong's team. A slender and vulnerable-looking Spaniard had been taken on as leader. Then Armstrong said he wanted to ride and Alberto Contador was demoted to "joint leader." The description needs quote marks because the manager, Johan Bruyneel, had been Armstrong's alter ego for close on a decade. They weren't quite joined at the hip but each depended on the other.

However Bruyneel saw the arrangement when he wasn't talking to the press, Contador saw "joint leader" as just that, that he too was the leader. The two settled into an armed truce, neither attacking the other, neither supporting either. Then Contador rode away in the mountains. The following morning television happened to have an appointment to film the team's morning conference. Newspapers were reporting that Armstrong and Contador no longer speaking except to shout at each other, that Contador was an outcast within the team, that Bruyneel didn't go to his press conferences, didn't give him lifts in the team car.

"You're a winner, Alberto," Bruyneel started his morning conference, his discomfort obvious. Nobody smiled. Nobody congratulated him. Nobody looked at him. The camera pulled back to show Armstrong more interested in sending a text message.

"It's because of Armstrong that the Tour was televised live in the US," Leblanc said shortly after retiring. "The Tour was magnified ten times across the world. It was phenomenal. He also brought with him the world of celebrities: stars, singers, actors." So much had changed since 1993, when Yann Le Moëner, head of TV rights at the Tour, said he had *paid* a television station in the USA to broadcast the race. The change is well demonstrated by Bernard Hinault. Only five countries could watch him live when he won his first Tour in 1978. By the time he rode his last in 1986, the number had risen to 27, with snatches showed in more. By 2009 the Tour was on television in 186 countries. Not bad, given that there are only 200 nations.

Leblanc could see that when he threw out the little sponsors and introduced his "club" of "partners". Among the minnows who suffered were Évian, Perrier and Vittel, bottlers of water who fought to have riders pictured with the right bottle in their hand. Évian provided the riders' bidons; Vittel got the Tour to start in its home town; Perrier employed men to push green bottles into riders' hands and to stand in sight of the camera, their prominent caps bearing the company name.

In 1986, however, an American came second: Greg LeMond. American reporters still felt the need to write "bicycle race" after the words "Tour de France" but they were at least talking of a sport for so long a mystery to them. The cozy world of French drink suppliers found Coca-Cola outbidding them all, and for twelve years. The main sponsors remain largely French—a bank for the yellow jersey, a water company (Vittel revitalized and back after Coke found the fizz ran out) for the stage winner, a supermarket for the best climber, a horse-betting chain for the sprinter. But the stakes have changed. Vittel and its Aquarel partner have since 1992 been part of the Swiss multinational, Nestlé. LCL, the bank behind the yellow jersey, is not simply Crédit Lyonnais, which previously loaned its name; it is the international wing of Crédit Lyonnais with activities in North America, Africa and Asia, in 1972 the first western bank to open in Moscow. We are a long way from Guy Merlin and his seaside apartments.

Leblanc called Armstrong's seven successive wins—each without doubt, illness or serious crashes—"a domination of steel, metallic, like there was nothing to it. I don't question his seven victories. You have a guy who has rubbed shoulders with death, who had to put up a tremendous fight, with the result that he thinks 'I conquered death, I am stronger in my mind, I am more motivated against my adversaries.' That makes sense to me. Even today.

"I remember 1995, when Armstrong wasn't yet the star but a good team rider in the Motorola team. Fabio Casartelli, another Motorola rider, had a fatal crash, one of the worst memories of my career. Several days later, Armstrong won the stage to Limoges. I can avow that on that day, he won that stage for Casartelli. He attacked once, twice, five times, with a rage. I can still see him as he crossed the finish and gestured to the sky. I'm absolutely sure he was sincere, profoundly intent on rendering homage to his teammate. It wasn't theater. It was human.

"The guy wasn't insensitive. But in his job, when it was a question of professionalism, he went above and beyond what was required. And to do that, you can't be sentimental. He was right."

Leblanc denies saying his wins were questionable, as was reported in America. And he denies saying the Tour needed a better winner than Armstrong, to which Armstrong retorted that the Tour merited a better organizer than Leblanc.

"It hurt when he said that but I laugh about it now."

Leblanc was going to retire in 2004. He had worked enough years and paid enough contributions to the state to stop work a couple of years early. He decided after 1998 that he'd throw it in when he got to 60. That was 2004. "But then [the economy showed that] it wasn't the time to leave a career early—in fact, the opposite," he said. The president of Amaury Sport Organisation, Patrice Clerc, proposed a few more years and he accepted. He steadily handed over duties to Christian Prudhomme and then retired on the last day of 2006, when he was 62. Next year, in his honor, the Tour rode through Fontaine-au-Bois.

"People here will talk about that for a long time," he said. That day at their restored farm in the rue de Pont, he and his wife Nadine held a garden party for family and friends. They included Jan Janssen, his boss in the Bic team, and Janssen's wife Cora. They talked about the old days, often better by rosy memory as they are for all old-timers. For Leblanc some of the magic has gone since then.

"Modern cycling has become mechanized, conventional," he says. "The riders are now very close to each other in talent and nobody now can try to drop anyone on the flat. The average speed has gone up and the days when the big teams could let lesser teams have their day, as they did with the regional teams, have gone. The romance has gone."

For some, earpieces are the culprit. Surprise and initiative went as soon as managers could talk to their riders, they say. Marc Madiot, the former winner of Paris–Roubaix, is an outspoken opponent. "With earpieces, as soon as there's ten seconds' gap, the riders can react instantly. Before, you had to depend on Radio Tour to tell you who was in the break, until the blackboard man told you the lead, and then by the time the team manager could get to the head of the race [to advise his riders], the break had a minute. It's an element that kills the race."

Leblanc agreed. "Riders have become mere executors of their managers' commands," he said, "robots who don't take the initiative, who attack when they are told. For me, what makes cycling special and beautiful is human feeling, improvisation, and that is done away with. You can bet that when Marco Pantani went on the attack when the Tour left Courchevel in 2000, he didn't have his manager telling him to do it—and that's part of the beauty of cycling."

Armstrong dismissed Pantani as "an artist" for not using a radio, for riding as the will took him. But that is just what Leblanc and others wanted. Race officials tried to ban earpieces in 2009. A hope that it would be for all the race shrank to just an experiment. The result was a sullen stage and much grumbling. It was seen as worthwhile but disappointing for those in the Madiot camp, pointless and reactionary by the rest. A decision will have to be made but no longer by Leblanc. He can play his clarinet, go through the mayoral paperwork and help callers at the town hall and let others look after the shop.

"Do I miss the Tour?" he asks. "Not at all. It's in my past, a job I did that's over."

4

The Leader Of The Pack

Cyclists call a group of cyclists a *peloton*. Those who don't know, refer to a "pack". Every pack has a leader and none less than cycling, which is as feudal as a medieval dukedom. Tom Simpson as world champion sat and chatted with Jean-Marie, a lowly domestique, but that was an exception. A fellow Briton, Barry Hoban, was good for eight stage wins in the Tour. But he was in awe of the real *patrons* of the sport.

He said: "In those days the ace riders, especially the Anquetils, the Bahamontes, the Adornis of this world, Rik van Looy, they were almost like gods. I remember to this day the first time that Jacques Anquetil actually spoke to me. Bear in mind that we were all professionals. I just used to look at him—wow!—I daren't talk to him. He said something to me, I don't even remember now, but it was 'Anquetil spoke to me today! Wow, I've been touched.'

"There was an aura about these superstars which certainly isn't there today. They were larger than life and drove around in their big Mercedes cars. They always had, or what seemed to be, super-glamorous attractive wives. There was always this film-star image about them— they aquaplaned above the ground and we were mere mortals who groveled along.

"At a criterium, if we were eating beforehand, they would all eat together. We, the little lads, would all eat with our mates somewhere else. These guys were on a pedestal and were gentlemen as well compared to the antics of some riders today. They were always correct and a journalist's dream. The attitude was in being a real pro and I can remember my manager looking me up and down at one team presentation, saying: 'Your jacket is very smart, but your trousers are too short!'"

But it's inevitable he thinks his era more romantic than others. People who plan music for radio stations say the music we remember with greatest nostalgia is what we heard when we were seventeen. We were young but we were mature and yet we didn't have responsibilities, a mortgage to pay. Laurent Fignon called his autobiography *Nous étions jeunes et insouciants*—We Were Young and Carefree. For gray-tops in slippers, it's the Coppi era of the 1950s. For those in their fifties and sixties, it was Eddy Merckx. Now, it's Armstrong. They were the bosses.

Vin Denson, who rode as domestique to Rik van Looy, said the only tactic in the Solo team was that van Looy should win. When he felt the race was faster than he preferred, he shouted *"Piano! Piano!"* and everyone slowed down. Van Looy was the man everyone wanted in the criteriums that paid most of every riders' income. If some impertinent rider upset him, van Looy could exclude him as a condition of his own appearance. Whether that was true or not, it couldn't be ignored.

For two decades cycling was in the grip of three agents who controlled races, riders and sometimes their teams. It didn't pay to upset a star or an agent. Agents needed the stars but the minnows needed the agent. An agent tipped off by a star could leave a minor rider without races and drive him out of his living.

The agents were Jean van Buggenhout in Belgium and two Frenchmen, Daniel Dousset and Roger Piel. And at first they filled a need. Serge Laget at *Vélo* said: "In the euphoric world that followed the second world war, there were riders, roadmen, trackies, champions, trainers, soigneurs, organizers, spectators and managers. The same as before but denser and with more passion. Happily, there were a lot of riders, because everybody wanted to organize something, hold a party on the road or in a vélodrome, to show that life had started again. There weren't enough good riders to go round, however, since certain managers, profiting from the boom, unscrupulously 'sold' the young and handsome Louison Bobet several times the same day."

The result, said his brother Jean Bobet, was that one day Louison was riding at Fougères when he was also billed to be on two other tracks. "Managers did anything they liked," he said. Change was needed and change came. And, in turn, produced its own excess.

If you looked for a man to play a Mafia crook, you wouldn't be disappointed by Daniel Dousset. He was half Brazilian, short, dark, round-shouldered, spoke with a vocabulary thought not to exceed a hundred words. He was, however, honest. When he negotiated a contract, he stuck to it.

Dousset was born in Paris in 1917. He turned professional in 1946 for Mercier and raced until 1950. His little part in history is that the jersey he wore on the track inspired Félix Lévitan to cover the king of the mountains jersey in red polka dots. It was a near copy of the jersey that Dousset wore at the *Vélodrome d'Hiver*, where Lévitan was a regular in his youth. Dousset wore it to show he'd won the army sprint

In requiem: a monstrous concrete sports stadium stands where tires once hissed on the pink track of the Parc des Princes.

championship in 1939. It proved so striking that he wore it, too, in six-days. He also excelled behind big pacing motorcycles.

Jacques Goddet, who owned the *Vélodrome d'Hiver* as well as the *Parc des Princes*, was no stranger to unreliable deals offered by riders' managers. He needed a man to give his staff firm promises that riders would be there and they began to work through Dousset. Now set up as an agent, Dousset opened an office in the back room of a tobacconist's run by his wife and her mother not far from the *Vel' d'Hiv'*. There he hung posters from the six-days, installed a phone, and began to represent the blond-haired road sprinter, André Darrigade. And when Darrigade was pleased, others followed.

One of them was Brian Robinson, in 1955 the first Briton to finish the Tour and in 1958 the first English-speaker to win a stage. He agreed that Dousset was crafty, manipulative and greedy but that he was honest. "I don't think there will be many who got anything past him," he said.

Dousset wasn't the first agent, of course. Alphonse Baugé tied up deals for every Tour winner from 1909 to 1925. But Baugé was a team manager—primarily of Peugeot—and it didn't take others long to see they too could profit from dealing on their riders' behalf. From which came the excesses that opened the way for Dousset.

Dousset rarely made other than spoken agreements. But, "with the honesty of a horse-dealer" as one observer put it, he kept his word. Promoters got the riders, Dousset got their fees, the riders got their money. Dousset took ten percent, which is how he made his living, and picked up more by keeping the fees in his bank until the end of the year, when he settled accounts. His secretary was Georges Wambst, who won a gold medal in the team pursuit of the 1924 Olympic Games in Paris and then made a career in six-day races, of which he won four.

It's never been said what Dousset earned but since in a few years he was taking a tithe of just about every track, criterium and team contract in France, he raked in more than even the highest-paid riders. "Some riders loved him," the British rider Alan Ramsbottom told William Fotheringham, "but I could see how much he was creaming off. You'd be going to events and there'd be 60 riders, doing it day after day, and you'd think 'He's sat back there and we're doing this.'"

Dousset had Darrigade, Bobet, Jacques Anquetil, the world pursuit and hour champion Roger Rivière, and Fausto Coppi. He had Franco Bitossi, Federico Bahamontes, Felice Gimondi, Rik van Looy, Tom Simpson, Hugo Koblet, Ferdy Kübler, Jean Stablinski, Raphaël Géminiani and Rudi Altig. Plus every minor rider desperate to ride a criterium every day from the end of the Tour to the end of the season, just to make a living.

He had so many riders that he may even have been relieved when a rival, four years younger, opened business in opposition. Roger Piel had a long, friendly face with thick eyebrows and a mass of dark hair with a fashionable wave. Although younger than Dousset, he turned professional before him, racing from 1944 to 1954. He was national pursuit champion in 1946, 1949 and 1950 and second in the world championship of 1946. He rode, although never highly placed, Milan–San Remo, Paris–Tours, Paris–Roubaix and the Grand Prix des Nations on the road. It was when he stopped racing that he opened his agency.

The difference between the two men was marked. Dousset was short, dark and in the mold of "dass ma boy" boxing managers; Piel was quieter, dignified and formal, addressing his riders by the formal *vous* compared to Dousset's *tu*. That politeness appealed to Antonin Magne, who also addressed his riders as *vous*. Magne's Mercier team had good riders but few stars. Dousset couldn't sell them expensively and so they felt left out. Piel took them on and gained the reputation of the little guys' manager, head of the second division. Robinson said: "The difference between them was that Dousset captured the international riders, which was good for me as the only Brit, and Piel had the domestic market such as Poulidor and Anglade."

Piel's assistant wasn't an international like Wambst but a young journalist, Jean-Paul Ollivier, the man who became *Pollo-la-science* on television. But the turf war between Piel and Dousset pushed prices up. And Piel's relationship with Magne brought him his biggest prize: Raymond Poulidor. The rivalry between Poulidor and Anquetil split France. As Pierre Chany insisted, a husband once sat his wife on a heated stove for supporting the wrong man. Poulidor kept losing the Tour, mainly to Anquetil, but the more he lost the more popular he became and the more Piel could ask for his appearance.

"Poulidor always comes second, usually behind me," Anquetil complained, "and still they shout more for him than for me. If he loses, he doesn't have to find excuses. But if I come second or third, then I've failed."

The rivalry depended on not causing too much upset to Anquetil, for fear of killing a goose that laid such wonderful golden eggs, so Piel asked criterium promoters to pay more for Poulidor than Anquetil but to pass the difference to him in private. It got so that Anquetil wouldn't talk to Poulidor, that Anquetil, Dousset and Raphaël Géminiani, his team manager, were driven to extremes to compete. Géminiani, with Dousset's agreement, suggested Anquetil should attempt the impossible. If France wouldn't love him, it could be forced to admire him. And so in 1965 he rode and won the Dauphiné Libéré, again beating Poulidor, then flew to Bordeaux in a jet probably provided by the president, Charles de Gaulle. There he lined up to race the 556 kilometres of Bordeaux–Paris, which began that night.

The extent to which Dousset and Piel controlled and corrupted cycling showed in the Tour de France of 1959. The Tour was still for national teams and France was gifted. Bidot, the manager, had a wealth of riders but, playing to rules that nobody but an insider knew, picked a team mostly or wholly represented by Dousset. That explains why the national champion, Henry Anglade, was placed in a regional team, Centre-Midi. Anglade was with Piel.

So many stars in one team was as likely to be disruptive as productive. Anglade watched for gaps to appear and exploited them. He won the thirteenth stage into Aurillac, the coldest town in France, and moved to second place behind a Belgian, Jos Hoevenaars. From there the race moved to the Alps. Of the two star climbers, only Federico Bahamontes was well placed. He didn't need to respond when the other, Charly Gaul, attacked but doing so took him so far ahead of the field that he became the yellow jersey.

Anglade couldn't imagine beating Bahamontes in the mountains. But on the col du Petit St-Bernard he saw the Spaniard struggling in the mist and attacked. That took him up to the second group. That included Roger Rivière, who had stopped with a flat tire. Anglade attacked again, leaving Rivière and getting up to the leaders. Rivière got moving again just as Bahamontes reached him. The Spaniard was the better climber but Rivière held the world hour record. There was no better wheel to cling to for making up time.

And make up time was what Rivière did, because he couldn't face being beaten by his team leader, Anquetil. Bahamontes sat there like the pillion passenger on a motorbike. They didn't catch Anglade but they did wreck his chances of winning the Tour.

There was no reason the French should help Anglade because he was in a different team. He was also not popular with other riders, who considered him bossy. But there was no reason at all to make sure Bahamontes won instead. They could have attacked him. But they didn't. Why? Because the French were Dousset men and so was Bahamontes. Anglade was with Piel. If Anglade won, he would get better criterium contracts than the French and Dousset would pocket less commission. Bahamontes would also get more if he won, but Bahamontes was never at ease on fast corners. He was hard to better going up but his skill at coming down was so slight that in 1954 he ate an ice cream at the top of the Galibier rather than descend alone. He remembered crashing into a cactus on a similar descent; the thought of running off the road on the Galibier without anyone seeing was too frightening.

Bahamontes was therefore no threat to contracts for Anquetil, Rivière and the rest, and helping Bahamontes snubbed both Anglade and Piel. By the end fans had worked out what happened, although possibly not why. Anquetil was jeered at the *Parc des Princes*, Europeans whistling to show their contempt. Cynical to the end, always seeing cycling as business rather than sport, he bought a boat and called it *Sifflet* 59—The Whistle of '59.

It's worth asking—although there'll never be an answer—how many Tours Poulidor's allegiance to Piel cost him, especially once Anquetil had retired. Lucien Aimar won in 1966 after Anquetil left the race because a conspiracy prevented Poulidor's winning instead. Poulidor was popular with fans but riders considered him penny-pinching and a moaner who exploited his weakness in the press, where it was translated into bad luck. Aimar was a Dousset rider.

"There were said to be times," said Fotheringham, "when Dousset would effectively order the riders contracted to him to produce a certain result, or tell them to combine against a rider who was out of favor and prevent him winning." The bunch ganged up against Poulidor again in Paris–Nice in 1966. Anglade had every chance choked out of him by close marking in the national championship in 1965. Rudi Altig won the world championship in 1966, it has been alleged, because Dousset said he should.

Dousset died in October 1997, when he was 80, Piel in August 2002 at 81. But their reign ended long before. Cyrille Guimard, who won 94 races, including stages of the Tour between 1970 and 1974, stopped racing in 1976 and became a team manager. His employer was Gitane, which began in a stable southwest of Nantes in 1926 and appeared in the Tour de France from 1957. Gitane also made motorcycles, which interested the car-maker Renault sufficiently that it bought a third of the shares in 1974 and the rest two years later. Renault had been confiscated by the government because it made trucks for the Germans and so its staff and Gitane's managing director, a man called Loeuillet, were civil servants.

And when in 1976 one of his riders crashed and couldn't ride a criterium for which he had been contracted, Loeuillet realized the legal and employment problems. Who was liable if a rider representing Gitane didn't fulfill an engagement? Who was liable for a rider—an employee—when he fell ill or had a work accident? Guimard explained that riders were contracted through Piel. Loeuillet asked to meet him. Only those there know what was said but because of it Piel left, feeling undermined. Dousset was sympathetic because what happened to Piel could happen to him. The following year the two made their tour of riders' hotels during the rest day of the Tour, the time riders accepted criterium rides. This time Piel and Dousset refused to handle Gitane riders. It was then they paid for their duopoly. Their ban was an infringement of the right to work. Dousset and Piel washed away in the floodwater through the breach.

5
Shooting Stars

Cyclists are like everyone else. They get stage-struck and they grow overawed. Barry Hoban said: "The riders play into the hands of the greats. They played into the hands of Merckx, Indurain and Armstrong, in that they almost beat themselves. It's always been the case, the greats overawe the opposition, and the opposition start riding for second, third, fourth and fifth place. The Tour plays into the hands of the guy who's dominating."

Sometimes the organizers appear to help stars as they plan their route, at other times to plot against them. Sometimes they have told them to stay away. That happened in 2003 with Mario Cipollini, an Italian sprinter who entertained by dressing as a gladiator and saying he'd rather be a porn star but treated the Tour as individual races to be won in a rush for the line. Then he went home at the start of the mountains, which didn't suit him. He was riding a week-long race while others were trying to last a month.

Leblanc said: "He wanted to take us for idiots. He was world champion. He went to sell himself, that's to say, to sign a fantastic contract with a sponsor from whom he took, in my opinion, almost all the budget. Since there wasn't that much money left after that, the rest of the riders in his team weren't that good. I know that Cipollini had promised his sponsor, 'With me you'll do the Tour de France' [but] the 2003 Tour de France was pretty mountainous, and in any case the mountains began on the seventh stage. I knew very well that Cipollini would abandon on the seventh day. He never finished an edition of the Tour; he can't get over a big col. The Tour is not a hostage to the demands of a champion, no matter who he is."

Every year, at the presentation in Paris, journalists play the game of forecasting whom the course will favor, whom it was designed to eliminate. They only occasionally agree and they often get it wrong. In 1987, Goddet's last Tour and the first that Lévitan missed after being fired, Pierre Chany said it was designed as "a Tour for the Colombians" because it was the most mountainous since the days of Desgrange. Instead, only two Colombians were in the first ten. The better, Lucho Herrera was almost nine and a half minutes behind the winner, the cherubic Irishman Stephen Roche, who was nobody's forecast as a mountain goat.

Had the course been designed for wiry South Americans? Goddet wasn't likely to say. But he did say years after the event that he plotted in 1963 to end the supremacy of his own countryman, Jacques Anquetil. He was tired of his "morose" style. He never made an effort that didn't count, never led the Tour over a mountain, never troubled to learn the names of half the riders in the field. And when the time-trials came, he slid past the rest in a shower of sweat from his woolen jersey. Leblanc said: "Goddet told me they decided to reduce the time-trials. And what do you think happened? Anquetil won."

Martin Ayres, former editor of *Cycling*, remembered: "Until 1963, his Tour victories were based on superiority in the time-trials. Fans respect great time-trialists but their real affection is reserved for the mountain men. The 1963 Tour was a breakthrough for Anquetil. He won four stages: two time-trials and, for the first time, two mountain stages." He finished the Tour emaciated and with staring eyes because of what it had cost him, but he had won despite the race being planned against him. He had an uncanny relationship with time. To him, said his wife Janine, 3:01pm wasn't at all the same as 3pm. He wasn't being difficult: it just wasn't the same time. This, after all, was a man who enjoyed driving through a long sequence of traffic lights, calculating the exact speed to arrive at each as it turned green. If Goddet denied him time against the clock, he'd take it elsewhere.

Anquetil rode low on his bike, or at any rate the lower than the rest, feet pointed downwards, and crouched like an egg, the first rider to cheat wind resistance. His body moved in the same way as his tactics, with never a surplus movement. "He was the world's most beautiful pedaling machine," wrote Jean-Paul Ollivier. He could drop nobody but nobody could drop him.

At other times, it's been outsiders who've plotted against the Tour. For years, Gaston Defferre had been mayor of the southeastern city of Marseille. He ran it from 1944 to 1946, thanks to his reputation as a Resistance member from the early days of the war, and then from 1953 until he died in 1986. For much of that time he was also a deputy in the national government and sometimes a government minister.

He was, to say the least, colorful. Marseille has a rich cosmopolitan population as a port on the Mediterranean. Drug smugglers, drug-makers and the Mafia—sometimes the same people—were active there. Turkey sold its opium poppies to legitimate companies but the surplus reached the underworld through Marseille. The first heroin labs in the city were found in 1937. By 1960, as much as 2,300 kilo-grams of heroin was reaching the USA from Marseille every year. The so-called French Connection had up to 90 percent of the American market by 1969.

Deals had to be struck, winks and nods engaged in. It was never clear whether Defferre was implicated but a man who ran Marseille, became a government minister and dealt with the Mafia was likely to have a high opinion of himself. And it shows in a curious chronologi-cal gap in Marseille's history.

The Tour had a stage finish in the city almost every year from 1903 to 1957. There was then a gap while the city rebuilt itself and then the Tour started visiting again. Until 1971. After that there is a gap until 1989 that no reconstruction work can explain. So what happened? The answer is Luis Ocaña and his clash with Eddy Merckx, who had al-ready won the Tour in 1969 and 1970 and taken fourteen stages in the process. He won in 1969 by eighteen minutes. He looked unbeatable until Ocaña challenged him.

Luis Ocaña, a slight, dark, debonair man, was born in Priego de Córdoba, east of Madrid. A street there is named after him. When he was twelve his family moved to Mont-de-Marsan in southwest France. He bought a bicycle that year and at sixteen joined a club in nearby Aire-sur-l'Adour before moving to the club in Mont-de-Marsan. He lived in the area until he committed suicide in 1994.

When Barry Hoban said riders allowed themselves to be overawed and then beaten, he wasn't thinking of Ocaña. The little Spaniard went to the Tour in 1971 after winning the Tour of the Basque Country and after giving Merckx a tough time in the Dauphiné Libéré. Far from stage-struck, he attacked after seventeen kilometres on the stage through the Alps from Grenoble to Orcières-Merlette. The handful who went with him had dropped off by the col de Noyer at 74 kilometres.

Celestino Vercelli, a domestique in the Italian Scic team, remembered: "Merckx never let anybody break away. But that day…we don't know…The start was on an upgrade and he wasn't that brilliant in the beginning. Maybe he was still warming up and his adversaries, Luis Ocaña, Joaquim Agostinho, Joop Zoetemelk, noticed that and decided to break away immediately."

By the top of the Noyer, Ocaña had 5 minutes, 25 seconds on Merckx and the Belgian was begging the field to chase, shouting it was in everybody's interest. The field didn't agree. Jean-Paul Ollivier said of Merckx that "there were no clever tactics, no camouflage, tactical feints. From the first kilometres, often, other riders just knew what was going to happen." He let nobody win anything and when a little girl called him "a cannibal", the name stuck. Riders ended up racing for second place, often far behind, and sponsors were growing hard to find. Worse, promoters had to pay him so much start money that there were just crumbs for everyone else. Well, if Merckx was in trouble now, let's sit back and enjoy the moment.

Ocaña won the stage by almost nine minutes. "Things will never be the same again," Goddet wrote in *L'Équipe*. A rest day followed and the Tour restarted with Ocaña in the yellow jersey. And this is where Defferre comes into the story, because the stage went to Marseille. It began with a 20-kilometre descent that melted the glue holding many riders' tires to the rim because of the repeated braking, then continued 280 kilometres along a valley. Merckx told his team to attack from the start. Rini Wagtmans was the first and then, in the valley, Merckx went to the front for much of the rest.

Nobody who'd stopped to replace a melting tire got back on, including some of Merckx's own teammates. The Tour experienced some of its most spectacular hours. Among those listening to the radio was Defferre. He hadn't intended to go to the finish in the city's Old Port but he wasn't going to miss the chance to be seen with good news. He looked after other business and then went to the finish. Because he wasn't expected, nobody warned him the race was gaining more and more on its schedule. "We went so fast that when we arrived in Marseille there were no television cameras there to broadcast our arrival," said Vercelli. "We were two and a half hours early. So the finish was never filmed. At that time they usually showed only the last part of each stage on TV and we arrived before they could start doing that." The entire Kas team finished outside the time limit and were about to be sent home until they were reprieved.

Defferre arrived in mayoral pomp to find workmen clearing away the barriers. Even the officials had left for their hotels. He banned the Tour from coming to Marseille ever again. It didn't go back until 1989, three years after his death. It was the first time since the birth of the Tour and the ban on racing in Paris that the Tour had been expelled from a city. And it's still the only time.

As a footnote, the episode did wonders for the ski resort of Orcières-Merlette. "The day afterwards," say Jean-Luc Boeuf and Yves Léonard, "crowds of tourists went to discover the unknown place they had seen only on television."

6
English Not Spoken Here

The first Tours had a single language: French. There were riders from Belgium and Switzerland but French was a national language in both, even if not everybody spoke it well. The two Germans, Fischer and Bartelmann, talked among themselves. Only slowly did other nationalities take an interest, with a lone Italian in 1904. There were more Belgians and five Italians on the eve of the first world war but that was it, apart from two Australians, Duncan "Don" Kirkham and Iddo Munro, who made up two-thirds of the Phebus-Dunlop team.

Kirkham appears—it's not definite—to have been born in Lyndhurst, Victoria, on new year's day, 1887. He became one of Australia's most successful riders on the road and track, where he rode every distance up to six-days. Somehow the idea grew that Australia's best should ride the Tour of 1914. Kirkham, Munro, Charlie Snell, George Bell and Charlie Piercey sailed to Europe. There, say some reports, they found contracts with Gladiator-Dunlop in Paris. Others say it was only Munro.

The *Sidney Morning Herald* said of Kirkham: "Although at first considerably inconvenienced by the small gears used, he accustomed himself to the much more rapid pedaling and the different conditions in every way, and ran second in the Paris to Nancy race." The Australians also rode Milan–San Remo, the Tour of Belgium and Paris–Brussels. Their placings were good but didn't impress. They needed to join a team prepared to enter the Tour, and only Munro and Kirkham did it, riding for Phebus-Dunlop with its only other rider, Georges Passerieu. The three could talk easily: Passerieu, while French, had been born in England.

Munro came seventeenth and Kirkham twenty-fourth. The *Morning Herald* barely mentioned it. Kirkham's obituary contained a long list of other rides but the Tour was a faraway race of which journalists knew little. He went back to Australia when war broke out and carried on racing until 1925. He tried car racing but crashed, injuring himself. The paper doesn't say how he died but other reports insist he was knocked off by a drunken driver as he was cycling to his farm. He died from tuberculosis and pneumonia that followed delays in treatment.

Munro, who was born in a house beside the finish of the Melbourne–Warnambool Classic in which he set a record speed in 1909, opened a taxi business in Melbourne when he got home. Embassy Taxis still exists. He stayed in cycling and campaigned for racers to be allowed derailleur gears. He lived to 94, dying in 1984 in Coburg, Victoria.

The two Australians rode under Desgrange. The Tour was still open to whoever turned up. Desgrange hoped for the best but accepted the rest. By Goddet's era, there were nothing but invitations.

Goddet went to school in Britain and formed his ideas there about sport. The British team he enlisted in 1955 was a novelty for the Tour but a funeral bell for the British bike trade. It lived in a half-lit world in which it sold fewer and fewer bikes, made greater and greater losses and yet conducted its own funeral with pomp. Raleigh held its trade show at the Royal Albert Hall in Kensington, west London. Hercules booked the Piccadilly hotel in the West End. The men who ran the trade lived in the grandiose Thirties when there was still money to employ long-distance record-breakers to publicize their bikes. Now that they sold less than ever, they dreamed of running whole professional road teams.

What makes this more nonsensical is that the administration of the sport was also fighting to the death. Not against outsiders and their dwindling interest in bikes but over whether cycle-racing should be in secret to avoid public disapproval, whether races should be against the clock, or on the track, or in colorful bunches hurtling along public roads. There were three controlling bodies in England and Wales alone—Scotland had yet another—and their distrust and hatred meant none could be trusted to pick a team for the Tour. On top, each sponsor wanted more of its riders than those of other teams. In the end, the squad was picked by journalists recruited for the moment. And then, not knowing or not caring, they broke the rules.

William Fotheringham says in *Roule Britannia*: "There was vast potential for secret collusion between teammates who rode for the same commercial team for the rest of the year but were put in different national or regional teams for the Tour. The same…applied to professional team managers. If they ran national teams, there was every chance that they would favor their own riders, so the teams had to be directed by outsiders who did not work for a trade team. In 1955, the presence of Syd Cozens, manager of Hercules, at the helm of the Great Britain squad caused howls of protest among the French cycle trade, who felt the British were bending the rules." There was little he could do that would affect the French bike trade and its riders but if he could run a team then so should French managers.

Brian Robinson called Cozens "a bandit." He was a former track rider from Manchester in northern England. He came second in the world sprint championship in 1929 and 1930 and then turned professional to win the London six-day with Piet van Kempen of Holland in 1934. By the time of the Tour he had become what one writer called a bespectacled, Mr Pickwick figure. But he remained a track rider. If he raced on the road then it had been rarely and only alone against the clock. Why Hercules should pick such a man to run a team to ride Continental classics and form the backbone of a Tour squad is a mystery. But it was in keeping: he replaced Frank Southall, a track rider and an outstanding time-trialist but still a man who had never ridden a bunch race on anything but closed roads.

Was that odd? Seemingly not for the Dutch. They had a manager who had never raced on a freewheel, says Benjo Maso. By contrast, France had Marcel Bidot and Italy had Alfredo Binda. Bidot, who selected his team from notes made on cigarette packets—and was given an award by the tobacco industry as a result—had ridden every Tour from 1926 to 1930. Binda won the Giro d'Italia five times between 1925 and 1933. They knew of what they spoke.

The first British team were numbers 31 to 40—Dave Bedwell, Tony Hoar, Stan Jones, Fred Krebs, Bob Maitland, Ken Mitchell, Bernard Pusey, Brian Robinson, Ian Steel and Bev Wood. Most came from the Hercules team, which had spent the season on the Continent, and the rest from domestic teams. Pusey went on stage two, Wood on stage three along with Bedwell who never got back after a flat. Jones quit on stage seven, Steel on eight, Maitland on nine, and Krebs and Mitchell in the mountains on eleven. Just two got to Paris, Robinson twenty-ninth at 1 hour, 57 minutes, 10 seconds, and Hoar as *lanterne rouge* at 6 hours, 6 minutes, 1 second.

Hercules dropped its team and all its sponsorship within weeks of the finish. Robinson and Hoar handed in their mud-speckled bikes to be displayed at the London cycle show. And then they were fired along with the rest. Dennis Talbot, one of the team's riders, said: "There may be other versions of the story, but my understanding is that Hercules were faced with enormous costs and not enough receipts to make the books right. And they'd already been in problems with the tax people before, I think, and they weren't going to do it again by running the team another year."

It was the opening of a chaotic history of British teams in the Tour. Another rode in 1960, again with two finishers. Robinson was one and Tom Simpson the other. In 1961 it included an Irishman, not simply an Irishman living in London but an Irishman from Dublin, Shay Elliott, who held an Irish license. The team for 1967 included not only an Englishman who had lived so long outside the country that he couldn't speak English—Michael Wright—but a man who was as Australian as Elliott was Irish: Bill Lawrie. And still the lesson didn't sink in. In 1969 this Australian won the British pro championship. Officials belatedly acknowledged he had no right to ride but added: "We can't really take the title away from him now."

Long after Munro and Kirkham, long after Charles Holland, despite a British team in 1955, and the rise of Tom Simpson, the Tour still didn't believe in English-speakers. Geoffrey Nicholson remembered: "The cantankerous Louis Lapeyre, still press officer in 1976, had been so convinced that journalists from Britain were unable to drive on the right, follow simple instructions or fit in with the conventions of the Tour—in short were unsuited to be there at all—that at first he would only deal with them through an interpreter, the veteran English Tourist, J. B. Wadley. Even then he would have to be convinced that they spoke French before he issued them with certain standard press kit items like the race regulations and the prize list."

He would have despaired all the more at Britain's first trade team in 1989. The sponsor was a delivery company called ANC, initials of one of its founders, Anthony Capper, known as Tony. Capper was a chain smoker who weighed 127 kilograms, or 280 pounds. His team started the Tour and fell apart. He walked off, abandoned his riders, left bills unpaid, and vanished.

Lionel Birnie in *Cycling Weekly* said: "He was like a magpie, attracted by sparkling colors and dancing lights. He saw something, he wanted it. Capper was a gambler. Just as he couldn't walk past a fruit machine without slipping a few coins into the slot, so he couldn't pass up an opportunity to take on the establishment, beat the odds. He had an appetite for life that didn't just show itself on his waistline but in his vision of the future. All those calories he consumed sure gave him energy and drive."

Capper knew nothing about bike racing but he was intrigued by a letter from an unsponsored rider called Micky Morrison. He went to watch Morrison ride on the Isle of Wight, an island of the southern English coast. There, said Phil Griffiths, who became Capper's team manager, he saw the excitement of team cars jostling for position. "Capper found himself watching a car rally behind the race. He realized there was more to cycling than he'd thought. And he fell in love with it.

"He was a gambler. He'd spend the entire budget before the Milk Race [the Tour of Britain] and gamble that one of his riders would win it and that he could go back to the board and get another £100,000. And he did it. It worked. The man was a visionary, a poker player. But you had to ask him ten times for your money. Everyone who asked ten times got paid. But you did have to ask."

In 1986, Griffiths and Capper went to see the Tour. On Alpe d'Huez, Capper swooned: "This is where we're going to be next year. We're going to ride the Tour." Sentiment and advisors told him to pick British riders, because Britain was where his business was. But, Griffiths said, "the sponsor liked playing manager as well as sponsor and he took on riders who weren't suitable." So the team had two Frenchmen, a Czech, a New Zealander and an Australian. The start was in Berlin and ANC looked as though it had come from east of the Wall. They had no time-trial bikes and just four sets of disc wheels among nine riders. Hardly anyone made it to Paris. Before then, on the morning of July 23, Capper had squeezed into his car in the Alps and left his team to fend for itself. "He just turned his back and went," Griffiths says. "He just walked out of cycling."

Birnie said: "As riders quit the Tour, Capper invited guests, sponsors, potential sponsors and his wife and family to fill the hotel rooms left vacant. His wife smoked. His teenage sons had a knack of asking inappropriate questions, saying the wrong thing at the wrong time to tired riders who simply wanted to suffer in silence. Perhaps Capper was stung by this reaction. He should have paid the riders greater respect but perhaps he felt that as he had taken them to the Tour he, and his family, should have been cut a bit of slack. Maybe he took it personally or maybe he just felt he had failed."

That year he sold his share in ANC for £1 million. To lessen tax, he left the country. Nobody is sure what happened then but it seems he lost a lot of money in a harbourside development in Holland.

"Unbelievably," Griffiths says with deliberate irony, "Tony never quite committed his share of investments." Somebody apparently insisted he did. Capper, now poorer, returned to the transport business in Britain, then vanished again. The mystery has never been solved and at least one rider, Adrian Timmis, insists he still hasn't been paid. ANC was a product of the 1980s, one journalist summarized, "a perfect reflection of the brash, success-at-all-costs, don't-worry-about-tomorrow ethos of that decade. And just like many other successes of the period, when it came to the crunch it was underpinned by nothing more than hot air and empty bank accounts."

7

English Most Definitely Spoken Here

The first Americans to break through in modern Europe weren't men. Unnoticed even in the USA, an American woman came fifth in the world road race in Rome in 1968. Audrey McElmury, yet another Californian, rode on the track in America because there was nothing on the road for women. She trained at 4:30am and again later in the day, a régime she said wrecked her marriage to her first husband, Scott McElmury, a fellow bike rider she met when she was fifteen. The American federation was so little touched that it declined to pay her expenses to the following year's championship. Alice Kovler and James McCullagh said in *American Bicycle Racing*: "The argument against funding women was based essentially on the fact that there were so few of them competing and the dues [they paid to the federation] amounted to very little."

McElmury paid $1,000 to travel and stay in Brno, second city of Czechoslovakia. She crashed in the rain, got back to the field and rode off alone on a hill on the last lap. She won by a minute and ten seconds after 62 kilometres, so unexpected that it took half an hour to find a recording of the Star Spangled Banner to play at the ceremony.

The men had trouble even getting into races. One of their first was the Milk Race in 1974, with an English manager because nobody in the USA was available with experience. They came last, British fans despairing that they had been allowed to ride at all. Five years later, an American won.

"Matt Eaton," reported the *Pittsburgh Post-Gazette*, "was the scapegoat on the United States national cycling team. It seems that his coach, a native Pole called 'Eddie', did not like Eaton's 'rebellious' training methods. Eaton did not conform, so he lost his squad membership. 'There is a lot of politics in cycling. The coach pushed me off.' However, through his own politics, Eaton gained a spot on the US team which competed in Great Britain's Milk Race from May 22 through June 4. And he became the first American ever to win the world's second-most prestigious [amateur] competition. After completing the fourteen stages and 1,056 miles through Great Britain in 42 hours, 22 minutes, 23 seconds, Eaton looms as a US cycling legend.

"After the Milk Race results, 'Eddie' suddenly became an Eaton supporter. 'He was over the moon when I won. He was really, really happy. But then he commented to me that I still don't train right.'"

The British were intrigued that he had an English accent, Eaton having moved to the USA when he was eleven. But they weren't friendly. "People in England are biased against the Yanks," Eaton said, "and the English racers told me that I was not going to hold onto the jersey. Then, when I won, they wanted to claim half the victory since I was born in Great Britain."

The Eddie in the story was Eddie Borysewicz, a Polish coach who went to the Montreal Olympics in 1976 and crossed into the USA. There he joined a club in New Jersey and was recruited by the American federation. He moved to the Olympic Training Center in Squaw Valley, California, where, he said, he had to buy his own desk. For his first sessions he used a twelve-year-old as translator. He told all but one of the American team they were fat and had no idea of riding as a team. Aggravation was colossal, although Borysewicz missed much because he spoke so little English. And anyway there was no one else. Eventually he could fill lecture halls simply by being there. He transformed American cycling from a joke to stardom, although Americans never did master his surname—pronounced *borry-SHAY-vitz*—and called him "Eddie B."

Britain gathered something striking had happened but the French didn't. A team of eight in France in 1979 "wore cowboy clothes with broad-rimmed hats and rodeo trousers," *L'Équipe* reported, as mystified as it was offended. But then George Mount won the first stage of the Circuit de la Sarthe, riding against professionals, and Mark Pringle came second in the Tour de Loire-et-Cher in the same time as the winner, the Frenchman Michel Larpe. *L'Équipe* conceded that they had "a collective strength rich in promise for the future."

Borysewicz recognized LeMond as "a real diamond." Still a junior, LeMond went to Belgium, won a race almost every day for a week, then went home again leaving a nation openmouthed. Most foreigners struggle to get in the first twenty. At least they came from established cycling countries and there was a chance someone had heard of them. But nobody knew who the heck LeMond was and found it hard to believe he could be American, not with such a French name.

The American magazine, *Velo-News*, once ran features on facing pages about whether the future for riders with talent lay in America or Europe. The American camp was represented by one of the Stetina brothers, Wayne and Dale, who dominated the sport. The European argument was put by LeMond. Nobody outside America has heard of the Stetinas. They know all about LeMond. That sums up who won.

The change in atmosphere that Mount, Boyer and now LeMond brought led to the first American team in the Tour. The sponsor, a chain of convenience stores called 7–Eleven, started in Dallas, Texas, in 1927. Its headquarters are still there, managing over 8,000 shops in the USA and Canada. In 1981, the year that LeMond joined Renault, 7–Eleven supported an amateur team run by Jim Ochowitz, the husband of the world champion, Sheila Young. In 1985, 7–Eleven developed into a professional team. American riders have been in the Tour ever since.

The old press officer would be horrified, of course. French is still the language of the Tour and always will be, but English is its lingua franca. Few foreign riders speak neither French nor English. To the list of native speakers can be added more Irish—including two winners—and Australians, South Africans, a Zambian, New Zealanders, a Manxman, several Brits and Canadians. The only large English-speaking country never represented is India.

An Australian, Phil Anderson (born, like Matt Eaton, in Britain) wore the yellow jersey in 1981 and for more than a week the next year. The Tour was for the first time led by a rider from outside Europe. Sean Kelly, who never lost the air of the Irish farmer's boy that he was, won the points competition for the first of four times in 1982. A Scot, Robert Millar, won the mountains contest in 1984. LeMond won the

Tour in 1986, another Irishman, Stephen Roche in 1987, then LeMond again in 1989 and 1990.

Geoffrey Nicholson wrote: "By 1990 the members of the Foreign Legion were too numerous for any of them to be considered a curiosity. If a Canadian, Steve Bauer, was in the yellow jersey, then the rest had to treat him as a potential danger. The older nations—France, Belgium, Spain, Italy, Netherlands—still provided 129 men, roughly two thirds of the peloton, with thirty-five Frenchmen making up the biggest contingent, though none of them finished in the top dozen. Colombia had fourteen riders, Switzerland thirteen, and Russia, seven years after declining Lévitan's invitation, was there for the first time with ten."

Radio Tour is now in English as well as French. But more than the language has changed. Attitudes too. The author Graeme Fife recalled: "In the not-so-distant past, racing cyclists felt an obligation to take the whole calendar of races seriously. [Now they don't and] it is partly the fault of the sponsors who encourage their big stars to expend energy only on the main chance and to use many other races as training rides, pulling out after a few stages if it suits them."

Among those to suffer are some of the biggest, including the Tour of Spain, which has the misfortune of coming just before the world championship. Fife continued: "Merckx criticized LeMond on this very point: for lack of generosity with his talent. LeMond, answering back, slights Merckx for being envious of him because his brand of bikes sells better than Merckx's. Hoo ha. LeMond was, moreover, on record as saying that the peloton these days is full of riders as good as Merckx and, as if that weren't preposterous enough, claimed that the only reason why Merckx had the success he enjoyed was because he spent the entire pre-season period in preparation.

"Well, now, LeMond always did talk a good race, before and after the event. That Merckx was prodigiously generous with his talent cannot be refuted. His record of seven wins in the spring classic, Milan–San Remo, is unique anyway, but the very fact that Merckx was winning at the start of the year with a grueling calendar of races ahead is astounding. That and a punishing round of winter track meetings…"

LeMond's concentration on the Tour was nothing like Armstrong's. Lance Armstrong has many doubters in Europe but in the USA he is more than a champion: he came back from the near-dead. Recovery from cancer and the way Armstrong capitalized on it in running cancer charities, which in turn enhanced his image, spread cycling into heartland America. The guy with the six-pack and a beef jerky may still go to NASCAR races and the cyclists he sees may get an angry blast from his overpowered pickup but he knows an American had cancer of the balls and still screwed Europeans at their own game. Seven times in a row, buddy. That's worth another Budweiser. When Armstrong retired, said the *International Herald Tribune*, US television audiences fell 52 percent.

It had been Lance, and the Tour, and Lance-and-the-Tour. For all but *cognoscenti*, cycling was the Tour and the Tour was cycling. Armstrong did what he did for money and the money was in the Tour, not coming eighth with bleeding knees in Paris–Roubaix. So those who paid him wanted him to win the Tour, and when after seven Tours and a couple of years off he said he'd come back and do it again, a sponsor who'd never had any interest in the sport paid to advertise on his jersey.

In Europe, in world cycling, and in the Tour, it has had a marked and potentially dangerous effect. Of which more later.

8
Under New Management

Jean-Marie Leblanc ran the Tour from the end of the LeMond era to the end of Armstrong's, passing through five wins by the tall but impenetrable Miguel Indurain, with whom journalists struggled to find anything interesting in his life or personality. Leblanc lived through and grew older during the Festina scandal of 1998 and the disgrace of Jan Ullrich, for so long to Armstrong what Poulidor had been to Anquetil—but in the end taking the role of Anquetil when he was revealed as a drugs cheat and brought about the brief absence of German television from the Tour.

Now Leblanc helps run his village across the border from Belgium and amuses himself with his clarinet. A new man runs the shop: Christian Prudhomme. It's an interesting name for a tricky job. A *prudhomme* in French is an expert of his trade, wise and able. In legal circles, a *prudhomme* arbitrates between employers and workers. So far so good. On the other hand, Monsieur Prudhomme is a literary character of plump, foolish and wearying conformity. The Tour organizer prefers the first version.

Christian Prudhomme continues the almost unbroken tradition of having a journalist at the head of the Tour. His appointment surprised many because he was "just" a television commentator, alongside the former winner, Bernard Thévenet, on France 2 from 2000. But there are parallels with his predecessor. Leblanc studied in Lille and so did Prudhomme, at the *École Supérieure de Journalisme*, one of the oldest journalism schools in Europe. He was there from 1983 to 1985.

Like Leblanc, he followed the Tour on the radio as a child. He said: "There was a report at 100 kilometres to go on the radio and we were very happy to get the last fifteen kilometres live. Then I used to listen on Belgian radio to a man, I don't know if he's dead, called Luc Varenne, an extraordinary man. My father always listened to the radio and regularly to sport. I was nourished on that ever since I was tiny. Cycling has always made me dream, even if today, alas, it is in a mess. It is an extraordinary sport, a legend of a sport, a sport of legends."

Varenne has indeed died, in 2002. And he was extraordinary, too, as Prudhomme said, because he joined the Foreign Legion before the second world war and fought Rommel in the African desert. He got to London and, by winning a competition, began broadcasting to Belgium on the wartime service of the BBC. That led to making Belgium's first sports broadcasts, covering 30 Tours in a passionate, emotional style that never hid admiration for Eddy Merckx.

Prudhomme left college to work on trial for RTL, a national radio and TV chain. It didn't keep him on. His first link with Amaury Sport Organisation came in 1998, when it started *L'Équipe TV*. And from there he moved in 2000 to join public service television. On the eve of Paris–Roubaix in 2003, Leblanc asked if he was interested in being his deputy and eventually organizer. "Was I interested?" he said. "I just had one word—*oui*! It's not a job; it's a mission."

His dream, he told *Nice-Matin*, would be a repeat of 1989, when LeMond beat Fignon by eight seconds, overtaking him on the last day. He talked of flat northern stages becoming not sprinters' gifts but mini-classics, hints of the Tour of Flanders and Paris–Roubaix including cobbles. The return of Armstrong in 2009 interested but didn't excite him. The Tour lacked a leader, as it did after Anquetil and Merckx, but it didn't lack legend. "There won't be *fewer* spectators because Armstrong is there but the Tour is *complete* without him," he said. "For races like the Tour Down Under or the Tour of California, yes, he has a real impact, but not for the Tour."

Making Prudhomme heir to the crown upset some. In particular, it upset a square-faced, bespectacled man called Daniel Baal. He was the Tour's deputy organizer from 2001. From 1993 he had been president of the French federation, where he was considered an efficient if prickly administrator. The day Leblanc said he'd stay on at the Tour, without saying when he'd go, he pulled a rug from under Baal's feet. He and Leblanc didn't argue like Goddet and Lévitan but they were colleagues rather than friends. Denied a chance to take over when he thought he would, he gave three months' notice and left. Not just the Tour but cycling as a whole. He works now for a bank.

Anyone would be upset at having a dream denied. But Baal's dissatisfaction went further. He had lost faith in the sport. "We really need to stop taking people for idiots," he said in 2008. "The sport is no longer credible." This, after all, was the head of French cycling called to be judged—but cleared—at the trial into the Festina scandal. Festina brought dope controls tighter than ever but still the speed of the Tour kept rising…

Aside from Henri Pépin and his gentle potter between restaurants, every rider in the Tour has ridden as fast as he can or at any rate faster than the rider behind him. The winner may not have ridden flat out every minute in the 1930s but equally he didn't in the 1960s or the 1990s either. That makes it reasonably fair to compare the speeds of decades and to assume improvements have been due to greater health and natural selection—which is why records are broken—and because bikes are lighter, gears more numerous, roads superior and riders no longer have to mend their forks at a forge.

Rather than go back to 1930 or even 1913, start in the 1960s. That is the modern era; all but the tops of the highest mountains were surfaced, mechanics were allowed to help riders, team tactics were employed. It's as safe as statistics will allow, therefore, to start with the return to trade teams in 1962. In that year, Jacques Anquetil set a record average of 37.32 kilometres per hour. For most of two decades, if you take out exceptional spikes, it stayed within the bounds of changes to the route. If anything, it went down:

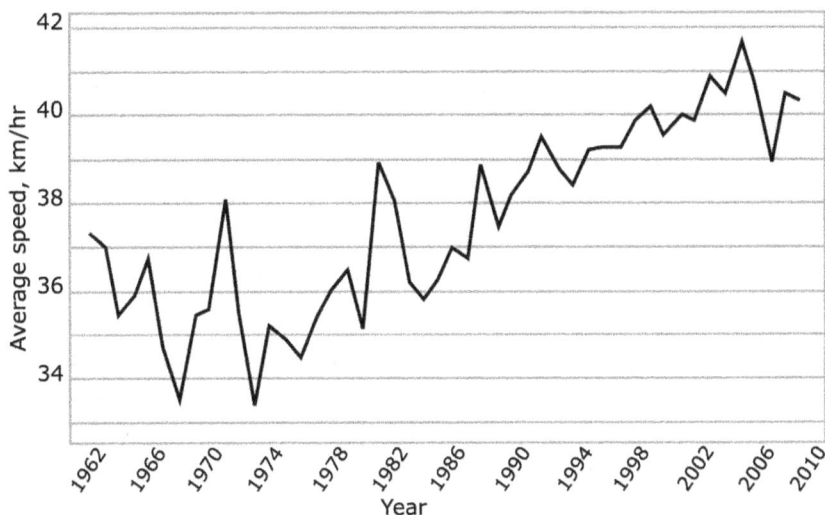

Les Woodland

Take out the exceptional peaks and it becomes clearer:

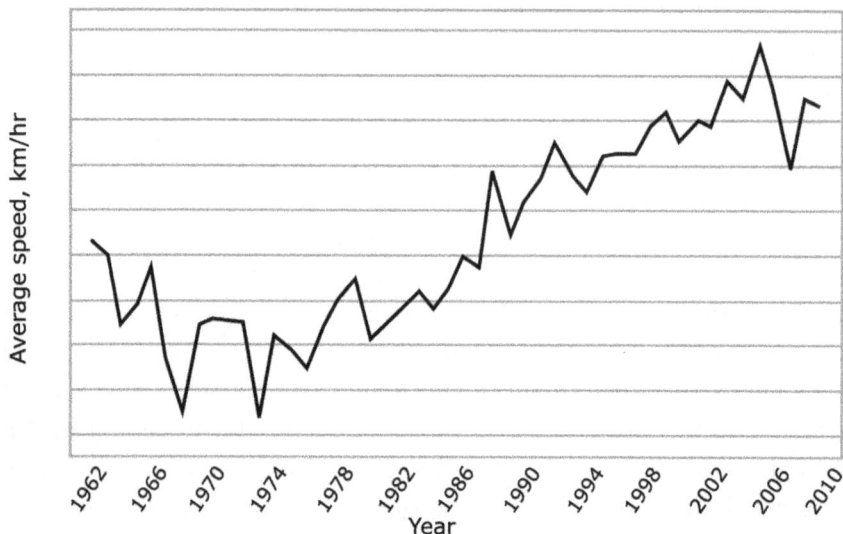

The average of the nineteen Tours from Anquetil in 1962 to Joop Zoetemelk in 1980 was 35.61 kilometres per hour, which was slower than Anquetil even though the Tour was 328 kilometres shorter. Zoetemelk finished in 35.14 kilometres per hour, fractionally slower than average. The following year was 38.96, ten percent faster. So what happened? What carried on happening, to make it 38.06 the following year? And what carried on until by 1998 it was 39.98?

While riders in the sixties frequently went slower than Anquetil, no winner of the Tour after 1981 ever rode slower than Zoetemelk. Between 1980 and 2006 the speed required to win the Tour rose from 35.14 kilometres per hour to 40.78. And yet the Tour was only 289 kilometres shorter—less than from Anquetil to Zoetemelk. That's an improvement of 16.5 percent in 26 years. The marathon record changed less than half that—6.2 percent—between Abebe Bikila in 1964 and Haile Gabreselassie in 2008, which is 24 years. The speed of the Tour rose 5.05 percent between 2000 and 2005 alone.

More than that, according to the *Institut de Recherche Biomedicale* (Irmes) at the French national sports center in Paris in July 2008, the Tour gets faster the more mountainous it becomes. Dividing the height gain of a Tour's mountains into its distance shows a gain in hilliness from 6 percent in 1960 to 12 percent in 2005, researchers said. In that time the winning speed rose from

37.21 kilometres per hour (35.47 kilometres per hour the previous year) to 41.65.

Armstrong and his drug-filled veins were part of it, of course. But only part. Because the speed has risen since then too. There are many puzzling sides to human endeavor generally and the Tour de France in particular.

Part seven: Le roi est mort, vive le roi!

The king is dead…Long live the king! The moment the fastest steps off the podium in the heart of Paris, he is "the former winner." The Tour has finished, gone. His glory grows already more distant. There were winners before him and there will be more after him. One day he will explain to those far younger that, yes, he once rode the Tour. And they will be bored, because he will be the generation of their grandfather, from the history of their school lessons. It has always been so. And it always will be.

Les Woodland

The most serious of Sunday papers in France is *Le Journal du Diman-che*, which means "The Sunday Paper." It began, like *L'Équipe*, after the war. Since then its analytical approach has earned it a place in serious-thinking France. Its opinion surveys are conducted by Ifop, the *Institut Français d'Opinion Publique*, founded after a professor at the Sorbonne in Paris met the pollster George Gallup in the USA. Ifop has become the heavyweight of French polling organizations and its assessments of politicians and policies are taken seriously. This underlines the worth of the survey in 2007, for the *Journal du Dimanche,* of how the French view their Tour. And the French, it seemed, line the road with few illusions. The paper summarized: "78 percent of them doubt the honesty of a victory, whether it's in the Tour de France or any other race."

Do you, personally, like the Tour de France?

	Total (%)	Men(%)	Women(%)
Yes	52	62	43
No	48	38	57

Today, when a rider wins a stage of the Tour de France or another cycling race, do you doubt the honesty of the victory?

	Total(%)
Yes	78
No	21
No opinion	1

Which of these opinions fits you better?

	Total (%)
The fight against doping in cycling should be conducted even more severely and cheats should be excluded from races, even if they are stars	80
Doping is now widespread in cycling; that should be recognized and it should be handled medically	19
No opinion	1

The *Journal du Dimanche* said the worry was that "only 36 percent of those younger than 35 say they like the Tour; it is older people who have kept their affection: 64 percent of those older than 50, 70 percent of those aged more than 65. Probably because this generation grew interested before the era of suspicion, whether it was individual (Pedro Delgado, contested winner in 1988) or generalized (starting with the Festina affair in 1998). Perhaps, too, because you have to go back three decades to find the last French riders in yellow in Paris, Laurent Fignon (1983) and Bernard Hinault (1985)."

Why? What does this mean? What else is there?

Graeme Fife spoke of divisions of cycle racing: "The men who concentrate on the Tour and nothing else and the real pros who honor the tradition of the sport." The last great stars to ride a whole season, with heart as well as legs, were Eddy Merckx and Bernard Hinault. The first not to, he reckoned, was Greg LeMond. And he was speaking before Lance Armstrong, Jan Ullrich and others.

The result of specialization parallels Mario Cipollini. He rode a seven-day Tour when everyone else rode a month. Those who concentrate on the Tour ride the same race but a different season. They hardly start from the same place. More than that, they force others to do the same, for there's no point in starting if you don't hope to win or have your leader win. The result is that even classics are becoming preparation for the Tour. And more and more specialists aren't riding those either.

The specialization rumbles more disastrously further down. The classics and Tours make up the visible part of the year. It would be disastrous if the classics lost their luster. But padding out the calendar and therefore the living of professionals in general are the little races, the Tours of this-that-and-the-other put on by clubs which every year scrape together the money. The more the stars, the more easily can the money be collected. But there are standing costs and a minimum prize list and so the price doesn't fall proportionately with the quality of the field. When sponsors lose interest in minnows, they keep their money in their wallet or choose another sport.

In France, the best of the rest are banded into a season-long competition called the Coupe de France. The hope is to create excitement and maintain interest. But, for all that the races are open to everyone, the field is almost all French with a handful from across the border if the race is near Belgium and a sprinkling of foreigners obliged to ride because they are in French teams. They are good races but...who cares?

Some of it is that no French rider has won the Tour de France in
decades. The last was Bernard Hinault in 1986, ending a period in
which Frenchmen won 20 of the 39 Tours since the war. An immediate
fall from a success rate of almost 50 percent to exactly zero doesn't go
unquestioned. And France asks the question over and over.

If you're not French, of course, it doesn't matter. You don't notice it.
But there are concerns for all. The more Americans won the Tour, the
more the sport succeeded in America. Belgium never had more new
riders than when Eddy Merckx won five Tours. British cycling, for so
long a secret society, conducted what one French commentator called
un holdup on the track at the Olympics—and turned the British Cycling
Federation from a damp rag to an organization with more members
than ever. A momentum increased again by finally winning the Tour.

Success breeds success. And defeat encourages defeat. Hinault's
club in Yffiniac, brimming in his day, has half a dozen members now.
Jacques Anquetil's club at Sotteville, across the river from Rouen, all
but vanished when he vanished. French cycling is in a dreadful state.
And while we may not know the reason, the consequences could be
worrying.

The Tour takes place on public roads. It is subsidized at public expense. It pays for police to escort it but there is local expense as towns
and cities lay on start and finish lines. There is no guarantee they will
make a profit and, when they do, it can only be guessed how much
business the race has brought. Along the way, a hundred communi-
ties a day are disrupted by having their thoroughfare closed, access
to shops and bars and filling stations with it, not just while the riders
pass but for hours before it. People can't get in and out of where they
live. Nobody can drive across what becomes a wall across the country,
moving on a little each day. It's all very well knowing that Gaston in the
village bar is selling more beer than usual but that counts little when
you're stopped from your daily life without recompense.

On Mont Ventoux, taxpayers pay to have eight tons of litter shifted
every summer, most, says the mayor, from cyclists and their followers.
The Tour is an expense to many more towns and communes than it is a
profit for others. Sponsorship may cover the main costs but they overlook all the incidental ones: the disruption, litter, damage, loss of trade,
minor road improvements, signposting of road closures, expenses for
planning meetings, medical care and much else.

The crowds for the Tour grow year by year, sometimes dropping, always making up what they lost. Nobody knows for sure because they can't be counted—claims for places like the Alpe d'Huez are preposterous because there just isn't that much room beside the road—but nobody denies they are a lot. The crowds turn the Tour into a national occasion, a month-long street party. But...

What happens when a politician questions, as one will, what right the sport has to clog up the roads of France in summer when only foreigners win? The logic isn't complete but the sentiment appeals. And it appeals to the many, as the *Journal du Dimanche*'s survey showed, who have no interest in the Tour. For the moment nobody has said it. But it would take only an analysis of the cost of disruption to start the questioning.

To question the Tour would be politically risky. Not everyone in France is a Tour fan—most are no more than generally interested—but there are enough that they're best left unprovoked when votes are at stake. To call off the Tour, therefore, is improbable. But what would it take for the government to say "Gentlemen, we lend you the roads of France at the expense of the French, but we get little back in national pride. You run a commercial company and you exist to make a profit. Perhaps the time has come to give back to France some of what it has given you. You can't, we know, guarantee a French winner. But let's say that we will give you the roads again each summer if you at least give us a French team. Please, go away, do what Henri Desgrange did in 1930 and give us something to cheer for."

Old Dezzie must be chuckling in his slumber. For the moment his Tour is safe. Perhaps it will always be safe. But, as perhaps you can now see, it never fails to surprise us.

Index

A

Abran, Georges 35, 38
Alcyon 67, 68, 70, 72-74, 76, 95
Amaury, Émilien 109, 115, 160
Amaury, Philippe 160, 173
Amaury Sport Organisation (ASO) 109, 161, 183, 212
ANC 202-204
Anglade, Henry... 150, 189, 190, 191
Anquetil, Jacques 8, 99, 113, 124, 125, 127, 133-137, 141, 150, 185, 188-191, 194, 211-214, 220
Armstrong, Lance 8, 164-167, 179-183, 186, 193, 208-212, 215, 219
Aubisque 51, 52, 55, 69, 102
Auschwitz 15, 107

B

Banino, Jules 56, 57, 58, 102
Barrès, Maurice 42
Bartali, Gino....99, 103, 119-124, 140
Bobet, Louison 99, 113, 127, 128, 160, 172, 186, 188
Borysewicz, Eddy 206, 207
Boyer, Jonathan 90, 91, 150-153, 163-165, 207
Brambilla, Pierre 118
Buffalo Vélodrome 14-17, 62
Buffalo Bill 14, 15

C

Capper, Anthony (Tony).... 203, 204
Chany, Pierre 19, 71, 77, 95, 106, 121, 122, 125, 131, 134, 141, 189, 194
Cipollini, Mario 100, 193, 219
Clerc, Clovis 13, 14, 183
Contador, Alberto 22, 181
Coppi, Fausto 90, 99, 118, 119, 122-124, 140, 141, 186, 188

D

Dargassies, Jean 36-38, 40, 58, 59
de Coubertin, Pierre 11, 97
de Dion, Albert 26, 27, 29, 45
Deley, Jane (Jeanne) 96, 97
Desgrange, Henri 3, 5, 8, 13-17, 20, 26-31, 35-39, 41-45, 47, 49-52, 54-56, 59, 61, 63-65, 67-70, 72-77, 95-103, 117, 120, 140, 194, 200, 221
de Vivie, Paul 28, 49
Dewaele, Maurice 73, 74
Di Paco, Raffaele 99-101
Dousset, Daniel 186-192
Dreyfus, Alfred 11, 25, 26, 42, 98
Dumas, Pierre 130-132, 135
Duncan, Herbert 13, 14, 199

E

Eaton, Matt 205-207

F

Farman, Maurice 12, 13, 61
Festina 174-177, 179, 211, 213, 219
Feuillet, Ludo 68, 72, 76
Fignon, Laurent 117, 155, 164, 174, 186, 212, 219
Fischer, Josef 38, 44, 199

G

Gachon, Pierre 87-89
Garin, Maurice 30, 36, 38-40, 45-47, 67, 144, 167
Géminiani, Rafaël 122, 136, 141, 188, 189
Gentil, Edmond 67, 68, 75, 76, 95
Giffard, Pierre 26-29, 45
Gimondi, Felice....125, 149, 155, 188
Girardengo, Costante 63
Goddet, Jacques 8, 28, 31, 43, 75, 76, 82, 84, 87, 90, 96-99, 105-109, 114-116, 119, 120, 122, 127, 134, 137, 141, 142, 151, 155, 156-160, 164, 187, 194, 196, 200, 212

H

Hinault, Bernard 7, 151, 160, 181, 219, 220
Holland, Charles 84, 87-89, 99, 113, 143, 157, 201, 202, 204

I

Isolés 73, 102

L

L'Auto 27-29, 35-37, 39, 40, 42, 44, 45, 47, 52-56, 59, 67, 68, 74-76, 88, 89, 95, 96, 105, 106, 108, 109, 113, 114
League of American Wheelmen 19, 21, 81

Leblanc, Jean-Marie 8, 142, 171-177, 180-184, 193, 194, 211, 212
Leducq, André73, 74, 77, 95, 99, 101
Lefèvre, Géo 7, 29-31, 35-37, 39, 40, 45-47, 49, 67
LeMond, Greg 62, 163-165, 174, 182, 207, 208, 211, 212, 219
Le Parisien Libéré 109, 115, 141
L'Équipe 108, 109, 117, 118, 120, 135, 136, 141-143, 165-167, 172, 173, 180, 196, 206, 207, 212, 218
Leulliot, Jean 108, 113, 114, 127, 157, 159
Le Vélo 26, 29, 42, 45, 55
Lévitan, Félix 109, 127, 142, 151, 152, 155, 157-161, 171, 172, 187, 194, 208, 212
Loubet, Émile 26

M

Magnani, Joe 89-91
Magne, Antonin 73, 74, 94, 101, 102, 189
Magni, Fiornzo 122, 140, 141
Major Taylor 19, 22, 25, 81
Malléjac, Jean 131, 132, 175
Manchon, Henri 127, 128, 130
McElmury, Audrey 205
Mercier, Émile 39, 95, 141, 187, 189
Merckx, Eddy 62, 127, 172, 186, 193, 195, 196, 208, 212, 219, 220
Mont Ventoux 90, 131, 132, 220, 134, 135
Mount, George 91, 148-152, 163, 206, 207

N

National Cyclists Union (NCU) 19, 82-84
Nye, Peter 18, 19, 22, 81, 82, 148

O

Ocaña, Luis 171, 172, 195, 196
Ollivier, Jean-Paul 117-119, 123, 157, 189, 194, 196
Opperman, Hubert 71, 72

P

Parc des Princes 16, 20, 26, 27, 37, 41, 101, 109, 120, 187, 191
Pélissier, Charles 62, 63, 64, 65, 74, 95, 99, 100, 101
Pélissier, Francis 64, 74, 99-101
Pélissier, Henri 62-65, 74,
Pépin, Henri 58, 59, 213
Peragallo, A.M. 12, 13
Pétain, Philippe 106, 109
Petit-Breton, Lucien 17, 55, 62
Peugeot 50, 67, 68, 76, 139, 142, 143, 150, 188
Piel, Roger 186, 188-192
Pottier, René 50
Poulidor, Raymond .. 8, 95, 99, 114, 124, 125, 134, 135, 189, 191, 211
Prudhomme, Christian 183, 211, 212

R

Robic, Jean 113, 118, 121, 122
Robinson, Brian... 188, 189, 201, 202
Roussel, Bruno 175-177

S

Simpson, Tom 132, 134-139, 142,143, 148, 159, 172, 175, 185, 188, 202
Steinès, Alphonse 50-56

T

Touriste-routier 56, 102
Tourmalet 51-56, 68, 69, 100-102, 158

U

UCI 15, 55, 81, 82, 140, 141, 144, 165-167, 177, 178
Union Cycliste Internationale (UCI) . 15, 55, 81, 82, 140, 141, 144, 165-167, 177, 178

V

Vélodrome d'Hiver (Vel' d'Hiv') 41, 106-109, 127, 187
Vietto, René 94, 95, 102, 125
Voet, Willy 174, 175, 177

Z

Zimmerman, Augustus 11, 13, 14, 18, 19, 25

www.ingramcontent.com/pod-product-compliance
Lightning Source LLC
Chambersburg PA
CBHW021052090426
42738CB00006B/296